The Catholic Handbook for
Visiting the Sick and Homebound

2024
Year B

Michael S. Driscoll

J. Philip Horrigan

Keith McClellan

Stephen S. Wilbricht, csc

LITURGY TRAINING PUBLICATIONS

Nihil Obstat
Deacon David Keene, PHD
Chancellor
Archdiocese of Chicago
January 26, 2023

Imprimatur
Most Rev. Robert G. Casey
Vicar General
Archdiocese of Chicago
January 26, 2023

The *Nihil Obstat* and *Imprimatur* are declarations that the material is free from doctrinal or moral error, and thus is granted permission to publish in accordance with c. 827. No legal responsibility is assumed by the grant of this permission. No implication is contained herein that those who have granted the *Nihil Obstat* and *Imprimatur* agree with the content, opinions, or statements expressed.

Scripture texts used in this work are taken from the *Lectionary for Mass for Use in the Dioceses of the United States of America, second typical edition* copyright © 1970, 1986, 1997, 1998, 2001 Confraternity of Christian Doctrine, Inc., Washington, DC. Used with permission. All rights reserved. No part of this work may be reproduced or transmitted in any form or by any means, electronic or mechanical, including photocopying, recording, or by any information storage and retrieval system, without permission in writing from the copyright owner.

The English translation of "Visits to the Sick," "Communion of the Sick," and "Pastoral Care of the Dying" from *Pastoral Care of the Sick: Rites of Anointing and Viaticum* © 1982, International Commission on English in the Liturgy Corporation (ICEL); the English translation of the "Order of Blessing of the Sick" from *Book of Blessings* © 1988, ICEL; the English translation of Psalm Responses from *Lectionary for Mass* © 1969, 1981, 1997, International Commission on English in the Liturgy Corporation (ICEL); excerpts from the English translation of *Pastoral Care of the Sick: Rites of Anointing and Viaticum* © 1982, ICEL; the English translation of quoted prayers from *Book of Blessings* © 1987, ICEL; excerpts from the English translation of *The Roman Missal* © 2010, ICEL. All rights reserved. "Order of Blessing of a Person Suffering from Addiction or from Substance Abuse," "Order for the Blessing of a Victim of Crime or Oppression," and "Order for the Blessing of Parents after a Miscarriage" are taken from the *Book of Blessings*, additional blessings for use in the United States © 1988 United States Conference of Catholic Bishops. Used with permission. All rights reserved. No part of this work may be reproduced or transmitted in any form or by any means, electronic or mechanical, including photocopying, recording, or by any information storage and retrieval system, without permission in writing from the copyright owner.

THE CATHOLIC HANDBOOK FOR VISITING THE SICK AND HOMEBOUND 2024 © 2023 Archdiocese of Chicago: Liturgy Training Publications, 3949 South Racine Avenue, Chicago, IL 60609; 800-933-1800; fax: 800-933-7094; email: orders@ltp.org; website: www.LTP.org. All rights reserved.

This book was edited by Danielle A. Noe. Michael E. Novak was the production editor, Anna Manhart was the designer, and Matthew B. Clark was the production artist.

The interior art is by Sister Mary Grace Thul, OP.

Printed in the United States of America

ISBN: 978-1-61671-709-4

VS24

Contents

Introduction 1

The Rites

Orders for the Blessing of the Sick 24
    Order for the Blessing of Adults. 25
    Order for the Blessing of Children. 32

**Order for the Blessing of a Person Suffering
from Addiction or from Substance Abuse 35**

Order for the Blessing of a Victim of Crime or Oppression . . 44

Order for the Blessing of Parents after a Miscarriage 52

Pastoral Care of the Sick 61
    Visits to the Sick. 65
    Visits to a Sick Child 72
    Communion of the Sick 77
        Communion in Ordinary Circumstances. 80
        Communion in a Hospital or Institution 88

Pastoral Care of the Dying 93
    Celebration of Viaticum 98
        Viaticum outside Mass. 102
    Commendation of the Dying. 111
    Prayers for the Dead. 130

The Gospels and Explanations of the Readings

Advent

December 3, 2023
First Sunday of Advent 136

December 8, 2023
*Solemnity of the Immaculate Conception
of the Blessed Virgin Mary* 137

December 10, 2023
Second Sunday of Advent 139

December 17, 2023
Third Sunday of Advent 140

December 24, 2023
Fourth Sunday of Advent 142

Christmas Time

December 24 or 25, 2023
Solemnity of the Nativity of the Lord 144

December 31, 2023
Feast of the Holy Family of Jesus, Mary, and Joseph 146

January 7, 2024
Solemnity of the Epiphany of the Lord......................... 147

Ordinary Time during the Winter

January 14, 2024
Second Sunday in Ordinary Time 149

January 21, 2024
Third Sunday in Ordinary Time.............................. 151

January 28, 2024
Fourth Sunday in Ordinary Time 152

February 4, 2024
Fifth Sunday in Ordinary Time 153

February 11, 2024
Sixth Sunday in Ordinary Time............................... 155

Lent

February 18, 2024
First Sunday of Lent 157

February 25, 2024
Second Sunday of Lent 158

March 3, 2024
Third Sunday of Lent....................................... 159

March 10, 2024
Fourth Sunday of Lent...................................... 161

March 17, 2024
Fifth Sunday of Lent 162

March 24, 2024
Palm Sunday of the Passion of the Lord....................... 164

Easter Time

March 31, 2024
Easter Sunday of the Resurrection of the Lord 166

April 7, 2024
Second Sunday of Easter (or Sunday of Divine Mercy)............ 168

April 14, 2024
Third Sunday of Easter 170

April 21, 2024
Fourth Sunday of Easter 172

April 28, 2024
Fifth Sunday of Easter 173

May 5, 2024
Sixth Sunday of Easter 174

May 9 or May 12, 2024
Solemnity of the Ascension of the Lord 176

May 12, 2024
Seventh Sunday of Easter 177

May 19, 2024
Solemnity of Pentecost 179

Ordinary Time during the Summer and Fall

May 26, 2024
Solemnity of the Most Holy Trinity 180

June 2, 2024
*Solemnity of the Most Holy Body and
Blood of Christ (Corpus Christi)* 181

June 9, 2024
Tenth Sunday in Ordinary Time 183

June 16, 2024
Eleventh Sunday in Ordinary Time 185

June 23, 2024
Twelfth Sunday in Ordinary Time 186

June 30, 2024
Thirteenth Sunday in Ordinary Time 188

July 7, 2024
Fourteenth Sunday in Ordinary Time 190

July 14, 2024
Fifteenth Sunday in Ordinary Time 191

July 21, 2024
Sixteenth Sunday in Ordinary Time 192

July 28, 2024
Seventeenth Sunday in Ordinary Time 193

August 4, 2024
Eighteenth Sunday in Ordinary Time 195

August 11, 2024
Nineteenth Sunday in Ordinary Time 197

August 15, 2024
Solemnity of the Assumption of the Blessed Virgin Mary 198

August 18, 2024
Twentieth Sunday in Ordinary Time 200

August 25, 2024
Twenty-First Sunday in Ordinary Time 202

September 1, 2024
Twenty-Second Sunday in Ordinary Time 204

September 8, 2024
Twenty-Third Sunday in Ordinary Time 206

September 15, 2024
Twenty-Fourth Sunday in Ordinary Time 207

September 22, 2024
Twenty-Fifth Sunday in Ordinary Time 209

September 29, 2024
Twenty-Sixth Sunday in Ordinary Time 210

October 6, 2024
Twenty-Seventh Sunday in Ordinary Time 212

October 13, 2024
Twenty-Eighth Sunday in Ordinary Time 214

October 20, 2024
Twenty-Ninth Sunday in Ordinary Time 216

October 27, 2024
Thirtieth Sunday in Ordinary Time 217

November 1, 2024
Solemnity of All Saints 218

November 3, 2024
Thirty-First Sunday in Ordinary Time 220

November 10, 2024
Thirty-Second Sunday in Ordinary Time 221

November 17, 2024
Thirty-Third Sunday in Ordinary Time 222

November 24, 2024
Solemnity of Our Lord Jesus Christ, King of the Universe 224

PATRON SAINTS   225

Introduction

Come to me, all you who labor and are burdened, and I will give you rest. Take my yoke upon you and learn from me, for I am meek and humble of heart; and you will find rest for yourselves. For my yoke is easy, and my burden light.
—Matthew 11:28–30

Suffering wears a thousand faces, and every face is Christ's. When we suffer sickness, loss, violence, or the harsher effects of aging in ourselves or in those we love, we cannot really understand the reasons, but we can choose the rock on which we will stand. We are members of the Body of Christ. Christ our Head is present in our suffering. In our dying we share his death. His voyage through death to the glory of the resurrection becomes our journey. In him, we are held securely in the face of the anxiety, fear, anger, guilt, and grief that sickness, aging, or suffering can bring.

One of the deepest causes of suffering experienced by those whom sickness or aging confines to the narrow world of home, hospital, or geriatric facility is a sense of isolation. We may feel misunderstood, rejected, abandoned by the healthy world of which we were a part, even by those who love us, even by God. We feel that there is something wrong with us. We feel no longer useful. We cause other people discomfort and inconvenience. We may know how we "ought" to pray in times of suffering, but we can't seem to do it. We can't even go to church.

When we have suffered traumatic loss or violence, we may suffer a similar sense of loneliness. Our experience has set us apart. We may feel that no one can understand what we have endured. We find ourselves unable to take an interest in the world of everyday concerns about which others are busy. We may even find ourselves ill at ease with our ordinary companions in faith and worship. Even God may seem to have withdrawn to a safe distance. Our usual forms of prayer no longer seem to suffice. We have questions that are difficult to answer: Why me? Why has God allowed this to happen? We may be angry with God and ashamed of our anger. On the other hand, we may find ourselves more deeply in communion with the suffering Christ or with his bereaved and sorrowful Mother than before, yet separated from others by the intensity of our spiritual experience.

Ministers of care, both lay and the ordained, are sent to step across the chasm that isolates the sufferers, bringing them the comfort of personal presence and prayer. Ministries of care are as diverse as the parishes that sponsor them. Some parishes may have full-time lay pastoral associates or other employees who specialize in pastoral care. These laypeople may have been specially trained. They may have participated in pastoral care internships (Clinical Pastoral Education), or sought degrees in pastoral care or received diocesan or national certification. Parishes may also be fortunate enough to have volunteers who provide pastoral care to those in hospitals, hospices, nursing homes, prisons, police stations, crisis centers, and to those who are dying or have lost a loved one. These volunteers can provide music, proclaim Scripture, offer words of consolation and hope, or simply give the gift of silent presence.

The most familiar ministry of care is that of extraordinary minister of Holy Communion. The word *extraordinary* can be confusing. In this case, the Church uses it officially to distinguish between ordained bishops, priests, and deacons, who are the *ordinary* ministers of Holy Communion, and specially commissioned laypeople who fill the gaps, so to speak, when there are not enough ordinary ministers to give Holy Communion to everyone at Mass or to take Holy Communion to the sick and the homebound. The words *extraordinary* and *ordinary* as they are used here may seem odd because they recall a time when there were so many priests that there was no need for laypeople to take on this role.

This handbook is specially designed for the use of lay ministers of care, so it does not contain the rites for the sacraments of penance or the anointing of the sick, or the special prayers and blessings used by ordained bishops, priests, or deacons. All lay ministers who provide care to those who are sick, homebound, isolated, or suffering in some way will benefit from the contents of this book.

You, as a minister of care, have been called to be a sign and a bridge. Sent by the parish, you are the living witness that the community of faith and worship has not forgotten the absent sick, the invisible elderly, and the unseen sufferers. Praying with them as a representative of Christ living in the Church, you are a sign that God is and wants to be with them. You draw them back into awareness of their communion with the whole Body of Christ. They, and in many cases their caregivers, discover through you that they are not alone.

The Church has provided two official books containing a wealth of rites for those who visit, pray with, or bring Holy Communion to the sick, aging, dying, or others who are struggling with addiction, personal violence, or the loss of a child through miscarriage—especially those cut off from full participation in the liturgical life of their local Church or parish. These ritual books are called *Pastoral Care of the Sick: Rites of Anointing and Viaticum* and the *Book of Blessings*. *Pastoral Care of the Sick* contains rites specific to those who are sick and dying, providing orders of prayer for visits to the sick and for the Sacraments of Eucharist, Penance, and Anointing of the Sick. The *Book of Blessings* provides multiple orders of blessing for various needs and occasions. What you have in your hand, *The Catholic Handbook for Visiting the Sick and Homebound 2024* contains all of the rituals from *Pastoral Care of the Sick* and the *Book of Blessings* that can be used by laypeople when visiting the sick and the homebound. Everything you will need is right here! You will be able to use this book when you are sent to give Holy Communion to other parishioners or pray with those who are confined to their homes, to hospitals, or to geriatric centers; those who have suffered the traumatic loss of a child through miscarriage; those who suffer from addictions; and those who have been victims of violence. The most important resource you have as a minister, though, is your personal relationship with Christ, our healer and our Savior. You too are the face of Christ.

Using This Book

The Catholic Handbook for Visiting the Sick and Homebound 2024 will tell you what the Church asks of you, as her spokesperson, to say and do when you visit, pray with, or give Holy Communion to those who suffer. You need not worry about making up prayers—they are provided here for you! In fact, except where the rite itself calls for adaptation, you must use the prayers as they are written because they express the common faith of the Catholic Church to which we all committed ourselves in Baptism.

Contents of This Book

You, as a minister of care, will be called upon to offer those whom you visit an opportunity to benefit from the strengthening power of prayer by making use of one of the many rites and orders of prayer and blessing provided by the Church. This book contains everything you will need to give Holy Communion and lead further rites for praying with the sick and others who suffer for various reasons. The rites and prayers are divided into three sections:

- Orders for the Blessing of the Sick
- Pastoral Care of the Sick
- Section 3: Pastoral Care of the Dying

Each of these sections contains the official rites and orders of prayer as provided by the Church in both the *Book of Blessings* and *Pastoral Care of the Sick: Rites of Anointing and Viaticum*.

Blessings of and Visits to the Sick and Suffering

Visiting and Blessing the Sick. You may be sent to visit the sick simply to pray with them. However, sometimes you may be prepared to give Holy Communion, but you discover that those you are visiting are unable to receive for some reason. At still other times, you may be visiting Catholic patients in an institution, but others who are not Catholic recognize you as a minister and ask you to pray with them. You need not turn away, feeling that you have nothing to offer. These are just a few of the situations when you could use these rites for visiting the sick and the suffering—either to prepare them to receive Holy Communion during a later visit or simply to enable them to draw strength and comfort from the healing presence of Christ.

Titles of These Rites. Some clarification about the titles of the services contained in this book is needed to prevent confusion. The book titled *Pastoral Care of the Sick: Rites of Anointing and Viaticum* provides two rites for visiting the sick: "Visits to the Sick" and "Visits to a Sick Child." "Visits to the Sick" is used with adults. These two rites from *Pastoral Care of the Sick* are simple prayers for visiting the sick. The *Book of Blessings* also provides two rites. These two rites are "Order for the Blessing of Adults" and "Order for the Blessing of Children." Here the word "order" simply means "order of service." These two "orders" present an entire service of optional song, Scripture, prayer, and blessing.

The Rites. The "Orders for the Blessing of the Sick" begin with a simple sign of the cross and invitation to pray followed by a reading of the Word of God whereas "Visits to the Sick" begins with the reading. "Visits to the Sick" continues with the Lord's Prayer and a choice of concluding prayers designed to address some of the different circumstances in which the sick might find themselves. Consider your options in relation to the situation of the person you are visiting. If you happen to be visiting someone who isn't Catholic, you may use this order of service, but remember to remind them tactfully that Catholics end the Lord's Prayer after "deliver us from evil." If not, be prepared for them to add the longer ending, "for thine is the kingdom, the power and the glory" before the "Amen." Above all, you do not want to cause distress to anyone.

In the "Orders for the Blessing of the Sick," the Word of God may be followed with an explanation of the reading, then a litany of intercession. The Church urges the minister to encourage the sick to participate in Christ's redemptive work by uniting their sufferings to his and by praying for the needs of the world. Prayer for others is an effective antidote to the self-preoccupation to which sickness and aging can tempt us. Intercessions provide an excellent way to meet this need. You may allow participants the opportunity to add petitions of their own, but beware of causing embarrassment by prolonging the silence if it becomes clear that they have nothing to say.

Both the rites for "Visits to the Sick" and "Orders for the Blessing of the Sick" end with prayers of blessing which may be said over the person who is ill. The "Orders for the Blessing of the Sick" provides two prayers of blessing. The first option is for more than one person, whereas the second option is for a single individual. The rite stipulates that the minister is to make the sign of the cross on the forehead of the sick while saying the prayer. The gesture may be unexpected or unfamiliar, especially coming from a lay minister, so it is wise to let people know what you are preparing to do. The sign of the cross may be followed by a prayer for the protection of the Blessed Virgin Mary. The rite suggests singing a familiar Marian song. If music is unavailable, only sing if those you are visiting are able to participate.

"Orders for the Blessing of the Sick" and "Visits to the Sick" end with a concluding prayer. In both rites, the "lay minister invokes the Lord's blessing on the sick and all present by signing himself or herself with the sign of the cross."

"Visits to the Sick" includes two prayers of blessing, one for a sick person and one for the elderly. Please note that the lay minister does not make the same gesture as given in "Orders for the Blessing of the Sick." Simply say the prayer.

The "Order for the Blessing of Children" and "Visits to a Sick Child" follow the same pattern as those used for adults, but they use simpler language. You will have to decide which rite or order of blessing is appropriate to use with older children. A word of caution: Before you make the sign of the cross on the child's head during the blessing, it would be wise to alert parents or caregivers to see if they have any objections. It is also wise to explain this to the child. Remember that very sick children may have experienced unpleasant medical procedures and may fear the unexplained touch of an unfamiliar adult.

Visiting and Blessing Those Who Suffer. *The Catholic Handbook for Visiting the Sick and Homebound 2024* includes three additional services for blessing those who suffer and may not be able to participate in Sunday Eucharist:

- Blessing a Person Suffering from Addiction or from Substance Abuse
- Blessing a Victim of Crime or Oppression
- Blessing Parents after a Miscarriage

You may meet people in need of one of these special blessings. You may meet them in a health care setting. For example, a patient may have been hospitalized as a result of addictive behavior or alcohol and drug abuse. Sometimes you may meet a patient who has suffered personal violence, such as domestic abuse, rape, a drive-by shooting, injuries sustained in an accident caused by a drunk driver or at the hands of those engaged in criminal activities such as robbery, or a person afflicted with posttraumatic stress disorder. You may also find that a woman has suffered a miscarriage, and she and the father are grieving together. You may also find people among the families of those you are visiting who ask you to pray with them or give them Holy Communion at home or in an institutional environment. An elderly person might indicate a child or grandchild who is suffering one of these needs and ask you to pray with them. You may be among those assigned to special ministries of care in settings such as support groups.

Be aware that the reason for the need may be recent or long standing. Sometimes, someone who is coping with illness, confinement in a geriatric facility, or other situation which has brought you to them will want to discuss something that happened long ago and continues to haunt them. Periods of inactivity brought on by sickness or aging give us plenty of time to think and may spur us to make peace with the past in a new way. These orders of blessing offer that opportunity.

Whenever you meet someone in one of these situations, you may use the appropriate order of blessing from the pages that follow. All of them follow the same pattern: an introductory rite (sign of the cross, simple greeting, optional introduction), reading and response, including the opportunity to comment on the reading, intercessions, the Lord's Prayer, a prayer of blessing directed to the particular needs of participants, and a concluding rite (general blessing). The Church encourages adaptation, provided the order of service is followed and the major elements included. For example, you might want to personalize the opening introduction, following the general pattern of the one provided here. Here is one example of a personalized introduction to the "Order for Blessing a Victim of Crime or Oppression." Imagine that you are praying with and for a young woman who is a victim of date rape. You might say something like this:

> God has always shown care and compassion for people who have suffered acts of violence, like the one that has brought you here. We commend you, [**N.**: *use the woman's name*], to God, who binds up all our wounds, heals us from the pain of betrayal, and restores us to our rightful dignity as a child of God.

The introduction now refers to the victim's own experience, uses her name, and avoids language that could summon up frightening images of being held by a male person.

You will want to choose those intercessions that are most appropriate. You may invite participants to add their own, and you may also do so. Turning one's own suffering into prayer for others is both a way of uniting oneself with the redemptive suffering of Christ and a means of turning one's attention outward. If you are accustomed to using the "Orders for the Blessing of the Sick," please note that there are some differences between them and these orders of blessing for those otherwise in distress. In particular, these latter orders call for the Lord's Prayer, which often provides the comfort of a familiar prayer; and they do not call for the minister to touch the person while saying the prayer of blessing for them. This can be an important courtesy when using this order for blessing with those who have suffered personal violence and shy away from being touched by strangers, even in prayers of blessing.

Like the "Orders for the Blessing of the Sick," these orders also provide a shorter form: a short invitation to prayer, a short reading, and a prayer of blessing. These short forms are particularly useful when ministering to those who have very recently experienced a crisis in addiction, an incident of violence, or a miscarriage, and are too distressed to concentrate on a longer ritual. They are also helpful when you are visiting the person for some other reason and find a need to help them deal with one of these issues.

One of the hidden benefits of the Church's rites of prayer is that they teach us to think in harmony with the Church. If you have never experienced the particular need for which you are blessing someone, your good intentions may sometimes stumble in trying to find the right words of comfort. It is easy to offend without meaning to by offering what sound like platitudes to those who are in the immediate throes of suffering. It is also easy to give impressions of God that hurt rather than help them. The texts of these rites will assist you to reflect on how to focus your comments. They are also impersonal enough that they offer room for participants in the rites to take them as words from God to be pondered and applied to their own experience rather than as personal remarks about their own faith response to what they have suffered. Ministers must be particularly careful not to suggest when they speak spontaneously that the sufferer is being punished for a lack of faith or for slack religious practice or for some particular sin. Remember that anger with God, fear of God, a sense of alienation from God, and particularly a sense of despair often lurk at the edges of suffering. You want to encourage instead turning to God in trust and in hope. Even there, though, please be careful to allow room for those who want to turn to God in a positive way but are not yet emotionally ready to do so. God's love is profoundly patient.

Holy Communion

This book provides two rites for lay ministers to give Holy Communion to the sick: "Communion in Ordinary Circumstances" and "Communion in a Hospital or Institution."

Communion in Ordinary Circumstances. The first form, called "Communion in Ordinary Circumstances," is especially useful if you are taking Holy Communion to the sick or aging in their homes. It assumes two things: First, that you have enough time to lead the full rite of Holy Communion, including a short Liturgy of the Word; second, that those you visit are well enough to participate in a full service. The Church urges us always to consider the needs of the sick or aging. If they are very weak or tire quickly, it's better to shorten or omit elements like the explanation after the reading or the Universal Prayer or Prayer of the Faithful, or simply to use the shorter form called "Communion in a Hospital or Institution" even in a home setting.

Communion in a Hospital or Institution. This second form, "Communion in a Hospital or Institution," provides a minimal format mainly intended for use when you are visiting many patients individually in an institutional setting. The Church expresses a strong preference for avoiding this abbreviated format even in an institution. Instead, it is suggested that, if possible, you gather several residents together in one or more areas and celebrate the full rite of "Communion in Ordinary Circumstances." If that is not possible, the Church recommends that you add elements from the fuller rite, such as the reading of the Word, unless participants are too weak. On the other hand, in the case of extremely sick people, you may shorten "Communion in a Hospital or Institution" by omitting as much of the rite as necessary. Try to include at least a greeting, the Lord's Prayer, the customary responses that precede Holy Communion itself, and the closing prayer.

Pastoral Care of the Dying

Viaticum, Holy Communion for the Dying. Any of the seriously ill, but especially hospice patients, may move more quickly than expected toward death. A person who faces death within days should receive Holy Communion under the form of Viaticum. *Viaticum* means something like "travel with you," but it is often translated as "food for the journey." Although the Sacrament of Anointing of the Sick strengthens us in the face of sickness, Eucharist as Viaticum is the sacrament that, together with Penance, prepares a person for the final journey through death to everlasting life in Christ. Catholics are obligated to receive Viaticum if possible. The Sacrament of Anointing of the Sick may be given after Penance but before Viaticum. If the person is unable to swallow, they may receive the Sacrament of Anointing from a priest instead of Viaticum; however, the Church teaches that Viaticum is the essential sacrament when we are in the face of death. The time for using the special comforting and strengthening prayers of the Rite of Viaticum to administer Holy Communion is while the person is still conscious and able to swallow. Once death has become imminent, dying persons may receive Viaticum every day for as long as they are able. An extraordinary minister of Holy Communion may and should give Viaticum to the dying. If the dying person has not received sacramental absolution, please make sure the person has the opportunity for both the Sacrament of Penance and, if desired, Anointing of the Sick.

Commendation for the Dying and Prayers for the Dead. While the sacraments, especially Viaticum, unite the dying with Christ in his passage from this life to the next, we also gather with the dying and those around them to sustain this union through the prayer and faith of the Church.

"Commendation for the Dying" does not follow a fixed pattern. You may select any texts from the prayers, litanies, aspirations, psalms, and readings, or you may use other familiar prayers, such as the Rosary. If you have had the opportunity to talk with the dying person and loved ones or others present, choose texts you think will sustain and strengthen them according to their spiritual needs and other circumstances. Pray the texts slowly and quietly, allowing ample opportunities for silence. You may repeat them as often as needed, especially prayers that have special meaning for those present. Even those who are unconscious and dying can sometimes hear more than we realize. If the dying cannot hear, loved ones present will find comfort in the prayers.

If you minister in an institutional setting, you may find that those who are not Catholic will ask you to pray with and for them. You may use these texts with and for any who are in need of the consolation of prayer. The texts drawn from the Bible are especially likely to bring comfort.

Once death has occurred, you will find both prayers for the dead and prayers for family and friends on page XX, "Prayers for the Dead."

Ritual Preparation. All of the rites are simple to follow. Look them over before making your visits in order to familiarize yourself with the order of prayer. Directions are included and parts are clearly marked so that you can easily lead the assembly in prayer.

The Gospel for Sundays and Holydays of Obligation

Following the rites is the Gospel for Sundays and Holydays of Obligation for Year B. The Church has a three-year cycle of readings. In 2024, the readings will be from Year B. It is recommended to use the Sunday Gospel during the rites for Holy Communion as one important way of uniting the communicants in spirit with the parish from which sickness or age has separated them.

In this book, the Gospel is clearly labeled by date and the title of particular observances so that you can easily find the appropriate reading. For example, if you make your visit during the Second Week of Lent, you will use the Gospel for the Second Sunday of Lent. In 2024, this Sunday of Lent is March 5. Simply look for the date and the title of the celebration and you will know which Gospel to use. For some observances, such as Palm Sunday, the Lectionary provides a longer and shorter form of the Gospel. For simplicity, only the shorter form is included in this resource.

If you are visiting on a Holyday of Obligation, use the Gospel prescribed for these days. You can also locate the Gospel for Holydays of Obligation by date and title. In the dioceses of the United States of America, the Holydays of Obligation occurring in the 2024 liturgical year are:

- Solemnity of the Immaculate Conception of the Blessed Virgin Mary (December 8, 2023)

- Solemnity of the Nativity of the Lord (December 24 or 24, 2023)

- Solemnity of the Ascension of the Lord (May 9 or 12, 2024)

- Solemnity of the Assumption of the Blessed Virgin Mary (August 15, 2024)

- Solemnity of All Saints (November 1, 2024)

If you are visiting very young sick children, you might want to obtain a copy of the appropriate reading from the *Lectionary for Masses with Children* from your parish. Another option is to read the Gospel passages recommended in "Visits to a Sick Child."

If you are praying with those who are struggling with addictions, the aftermath of violence, or with parents who have suffered the loss of a child through miscarriage, you will usually find the readings recommended in the orders of blessing more appropriate to their circumstances than the Gospel for the Sunday. However, if appropriate, feel free to use the Gospel for Sundays and Holydays of Obligation. To discern which readings to use, it is best to look over the order of service before the visit occurs.

Explanation of the Readings

You will notice that the rites offer an opportunity for the minister of care to give a brief explanation of the reading with special reference to the experience of those with whom you are praying and, where appropriate, of their caregivers. If you are using the Sunday or holyday reading, you might want to base your explanation of the reading on the parish Sunday Homily in order to deepen the sense of connection you are trying to encourage. If you feel uncomfortable about speaking, you will find a brief explanation of the reading after the Gospel for each Sunday and holyday. If you choose to read it from the book, it would be a good idea to ponder it and make it your own so that the words come from your heart and not merely from the page. The Word of God itself creates a bond between reader and hearers, breaking down the sense of isolation that afflicts sufferers. Explanatory words that are spoken, or even read, with sincerity and personal conviction will support this pastoral relationship more effectively than words read mechanically.

Patron Saints

Finally, there is a list of saints who the Church has identified as particular intercessors, companions, and guides for those suffering various kinds of afflictions, whether physical or emotional. If you feel that those with whom you pray would welcome the company and support of a saint, you might want to include the saint's name in the intercessions and suggest that those you are visiting continue to ask for the saint's help. An example of an intercession is:

> For all those who suffer from throat cancer, especially **N.** (*insert the name of the person or persons present*), that through the intercession of Saint Blaise, they may find comfort and strength, we pray to the Lord.

This book does not provide any information about the saints listed, but there are many books and websites where you can find their stories. Such resources are *Companion to the Calendar, Second Edition* (Liturgy Training Publications) and *Butler's Lives of the Saints* (published by The Liturgical Press).

Beyond the Book

The official rites offer appropriate prayers and clear directions, but they don't tell you everything you need to know in order to lead the rituals effectively. Here are some practical hints that may help.

Getting from the Parish Church to Your Pastoral Assignment

Scheduling a Visit. Some parishes assign ministers to visit particular people but encourage them to make their own arrangements regarding the day and time. Both those in need of your ministry and their families or caregivers, at home or in institutional facilities, appreciate being able to negotiate appropriate times for a pastoral visit or Holy Communion. It gives them an opportunity to make sure that they and those they would like to have present can be there. For example, if you're visiting the sick, you don't want to drop in when patients are absent from their rooms for tests or treatments.

If you are asked to take Holy Communion to the sick and the homebound at times other than during Sunday Mass, please make sure your training includes information about where to find the tabernacle key and how to approach the tabernacle reverently, open it, and transfer the hosts you will need from the ciborium in which they are kept to the container you will use to carry the Blessed Sacrament to the sick (see below). It is particularly important to arrange with the parish coordinator a convenient time for you to obtain the tabernacle key, because it is not permitted to keep the Eucharist at home or carry it all day as you go about your ordinary business before visiting communicants.

Ordinarily, when taking the Blessed Sacrament from the tabernacle, you would pray briefly before the tabernacle, wash your fingers in a small vessel of water that is usually kept beside the tabernacle for that purpose, wipe them on a finger towel also usually kept there, and genuflect after opening the tabernacle. If your parish does not provide either the small vessel or finger towel, wash your hands in the sacristy or otherwise clean your fingers as best you are able over the sacrarium (a sink flowing directly into the ground for water from purifications, from the first washings of the altar cloths, or the water containing the completely dissolved consecrated hosts which cannot be properly consumed).

If you have unused hosts left over at the end of your rounds, you must bring them back to the parish church and replace them in the tabernacle.

After closing the tabernacle, you again wash your fingers. You may also cleanse the empty pyx (a dignified vessel, often round, used to carry the consecrated host) in the sacrarium if it appears to contain crumbs. Fill it with water, drink the water, and dry the pyx carefully on a finger towel, if available.

If you wish to avoid having hosts that must be returned, you can give the last few communicants more than one host so that all the hosts are consumed or consume them yourself as part of the Communion Rite during your last visit, provided all the usual requirements for Holy Communion are met. However, you may not simply consume them yourself after your last visit because Holy Communion is always received in the context of public prayer rather than simply as a matter of convenience by the minister alone. Similarly, you may not take the remaining hosts home to return later to the church because the Eucharist must be kept in a tabernacle or other designated locked place of reservation in a church.

Bringing What You Need. Make a checklist of what you want to have with you before you leave home. You'll find some suggestions below. Don't forget this book! It does happen. If it does, don't panic, and don't fail to keep your appointment. As a precaution, make every effort to memorize the outline of the rites you expect to use or keep a copy of a simple outline in your pocket, wallet, or purse. In this case, do make up your own prayer, but keep it very short and simple. Borrow a Bible or summarize the Gospel in your own words. God works through all our weaknesses and mistakes.

Carrying the Blessed Sacrament. The Blessed Sacrament is carried in the pyx or in another dignified vessel reserved exclusively for that purpose. Your parish will probably supply you with what you need. Some pyxes can be worn or carried in a pouch on a cord around the neck. When you are carrying the Blessed Sacrament, remember and attend reverently to Christ, choosing your activities appropriately, without becoming artificially silent or stilted in your conversation, especially with those who are not aware of what you are carrying or of its significance. On the one hand, avoid distractions such as loud music, "talk" programs or other television shows, movies or DVDs/tapes, or other things that would disturb prayer while you are en route. On the other hand, while avoiding such distractions, be careful not to be rude to people who greet you or speak to you in passing as you walk to your destination. Christ is not offended by the company and conversation of human beings! You should make your Communion visit immediately upon leaving the Church.

Music Preparation. Sometimes it might be possible to incorporate music into your visits. Music most certainly can be included in the rites and orders of blessing. Singing familiar melodies and texts can be extremely comforting and healing to those who are suffering. Hospitals, nursing homes, and other facilities might have a piano or you might bring a guitar. A capella singing can be just as effective. Be sure to select music in which either the refrain is simple or the melodies are familiar. Choose texts that give a message of the hope we have in Christ. Here are some suggestions: "Blest Are They" (Haas), "Jesus, Heal Us" (Haas), "Healer of Our Every Ill" (Haugen), "Lord of All Hopefulness" (traditional), "I Heard the Voice of Jesus Say" (traditional), "Remember Your Love" (Balhoff), "Shepherd Me, O God" (Haugen), and "You Are Mine" (Haas).

Preparing an Environment for Prayer: Encountering Christ in Persons

Church ministry is always personal. It is important that you spend a few minutes at the beginning of your visit to get to know those present and give them a chance to feel comfortable with you. Your parish may be able to supply you with helpful information in advance.

When you arrive, put those present at ease by engaging in a few moments of personal conversation. Tell them your name and remind them that the parish has sent you. Ask how they are and listen attentively to their answers. If you are visiting the sick, show your interest and concern, but remember that you are not there to offer medical advice or to pass judgment on medical matters, even if you yourself are a professional medical caregiver. If you can, address those you are visiting by name, but be aware that not everyone likes to be addressed by a first name without permission. Sickness, debilitating aging, and other forms of public suffering often rob people of their sense of personal dignity, so treating people with respect is an important dimension of your ministry. Whatever their condition, you and they are both collaborators in Christ's work. Ministry is a two-way street: those whom you visit are serving you by their witness to Christ's suffering as much as you are serving them by offering them Christ's loving comfort. Take note of any special needs you see: is the sufferer low on energy, in pain, limited in motion, hard of hearing, angry, sad, or seemingly depressed? You will want to tailor the length, content, and style of the celebration accordingly.

Preparing Yourself to Lead Prayer

The world of the suffering, especially those confined to home or, even more so, to a hospital or geriatric facility may not feel much like a place of prayer. The most important element in creating an environment for prayer is you. The minister who prays while leading others in prayer is the most powerful invitation one can offer to those who need to be called from all the preoccupations of suffering into deeper awareness of the mystery of God present and acting in our midst.

Here are some steps you can take to develop this important skill:

- Devote time to praying, reading, and meditating on the texts of the prayers and readings provided in this book. You will best pray them in public if you have already prayed them many times in private.

- Familiarize yourself thoroughly with the structure and flow of the rites so that you can concentrate on the people rather than the book. You need not memorize prayers or readings. Simply know what comes next and where to find it.

- Before you go into the building or room, pray briefly, asking Christ to work through you; after the visit, pause to give thanks.

- Reflect on your experience after you return home. Were there moments during the celebration when you felt uncertain or distracted? Why? What could you do next time to make yourself more at ease so that you can pray more attentively without losing contact with those you are leading in prayer? Sharing experience with other ministers of care or parish staff can be a useful way to continue and deepen everyone's ministry formation.

Preparing the Room for Prayer

You can also take some simple steps to establish an atmosphere that encourages prayer when circumstances allow. A small standing crucifix, cross, or icon heightens consciousness of Christ. Appropriate lighting can help, where possible. In an institutional setting, for example, a lamp or sunlight creates a more calming environment than do fluorescent lights. If you are taking Holy Communion to someone, take a small white cloth and a candle with you to prepare a place to put the pyx containing the Blessed Sacrament as a focus for the celebration as you lead the other prayers. (Be sure you have something with which to light the candle!) A corporal (traditionally a square, white, linen cloth upon which is placed sacred vessels holding the Blessed Sacrament) is not required, but if it is used, it is traditionally placed on top of another white cloth rather than on a bare surface. Caregivers familiar with the rite may have prepared a place in advance, but many will not.

Be aware of the restrictions you may face in a health care or geriatric facility. The rites for Holy Communion recommend that the minister be accompanied by a candle-bearer and place a candle on the table where the Blessed Sacrament will stand during the celebration, as described above. However, safety regulations usually forbid the use of open flames in institutions. Oxygen and other substances that might be in use are highly flammable. Moreover, you may not be able to find any appropriate surface other than a bedside table or night stand that will have to be cleared before you can set up a place for the Blessed Sacrament. Be prepared to make whatever practical adjustments the circumstances require. If you have never visited a particular hospital unit or nursing home, see if you can find another minister who has and find out what to expect.

Preparing Participants for Prayer

After a few moments of conversation, find a graceful way to end the social part of the visit without seeming uninterested or abrupt. Then give the participants a simple, brief overview of the rite you will be using so they will know what to expect, unless you know they are already familiar with the rite. Surprises tend to disrupt prayer! It's especially important to decide in advance who will do the reading. The directions say that the reading may be done "by one of those present or by the minister." If you don't know the participants, the best solution might be to ask for a volunteer (and allow the volunteer a few moments to prepare), but remember that not everyone is willing or able to read in public with short notice, especially in times of distress. Finally, mark the beginning of prayer clearly by inviting silent attentiveness, making the sign of the cross and moving into the service itself.

Recognizing the Recipient

You are ministering not only to those to whom the ritual is addressed but also to those around them, whether loved ones or caregivers. Be sure to include them by looking at them and speaking to them, as well as to the person who is your focus. When you are saying prayers of blessing over the sufferer, your attention is on that person alone, but all present are invited to join in the "Amen" that affirms and concludes the prayer. Practice with another minister until you can say prayers in such a way that others know when and how to respond without having a book in front of them.

Who May Receive Holy Communion?

Catholic shut-ins, caregivers, or others who assemble with them may receive Holy Communion provided the usual conditions have been met. You can offer that invitation before you begin the rite for Holy Communion, being careful not to embarrass or offend those who are not eligible to receive. "The elderly, the infirm and those who care for them can receive the Holy Eucharist even if they have eaten something within the preceding hour" (*Code of Canon Law*, 919 §2).

Special Circumstances

Unfortunately, neither sickness nor the deterioration sometimes brought on by aging is neat or predictable. The physical, psychological, and spiritual condition of those you visit may have changed since the arrangements for your visit were made. You may need to make unprepared changes in the rite or blessing you are using to meet the current need.

Special Circumstances for Extraordinary Ministers of Holy Communion

If you are taking Holy Communion to the sick or elderly, sometimes those you are visiting will express reluctance to receive. They may or may not want to tell you why. They might be embarrassed to say that they are too nauseated; they might feel alienated from God; they might need sacramental absolution but don't want to say so. You are obviously a person of generosity and compassion, or you wouldn't have volunteered to be an extraordinary minister of Holy Communion. However, a Holy Communion visit is not ordinarily the best time to identify and try to resolve serious personal or spiritual problems. Be aware of your status and of the vulnerability of the suffering: You represent the Church, and you have more power than you may realize to make others feel guilty by showing that you disapprove of their decision not to receive Holy Communion or by giving the impression that they have wasted your time. Remember that they are not rejecting you as a person. Rather, they are struggling with something deeper. Offer to pray with them, using the rites provided for visiting or blessing the sick. Invite them to enter more deeply into communion with the suffering and risen Christ who loves them. Let them know what pastoral resources are available to them: offer to return or to send another minister at a more convenient time; provide the parish phone number; offer to let the pastoral staff know that they would like a priest to visit, without forcing them to reply. If the parish distributes a bulletin during the weekend Masses, bring one along to leave with the person you are visiting.

Sometimes you may find that those you are visiting are unable to swallow easily. Consult medical caregivers. If they give permission, you may break the host into the smallest of pieces, place a piece on the person's tongue to dissolve, and follow with a glass of water to make swallowing possible. Be careful with crumbs when you break the host. The best thing to do is to break the host carefully over the pyx so that crumbs will fall into the pyx. If any crumbs fall on the cloth or table on which the pyx has been placed, moisten your finger, pick up all the crumbs very carefully, and consume them reverently.

You may even find that someone cannot ingest the host at all. In such cases, the person may receive the Blood of Christ, but that requires specialized vessels and procedures. Report the circumstances to your pastor, parish coordinator, or to the facility chaplain's office if the person is in a health care or geriatric facility. They will be able to give Holy Communion appropriately. In the meantime, use one of the rites for visiting or blessing the sick to give them the support of your presence and prayer.

Be aware that the hospitalized may not be permitted to take anything by mouth for a period of time prior to certain tests or treatments. Even a small piece of the host received at such times may cause medical personnel to cancel the planned procedure. If you see a sign that says "Nothing by mouth" or "NPO," initials for the Latin phrase *nil per os*, meaning the same thing, ask a member of the medical staff if you may administer Holy Communion, but expect a "no." In this case, too, you should still pray with the sick or aging, using one of the rites for visiting or blessing the sick. Remember that you still offer them the comfort of Christ's presence in his Word and through your own presence and that of the parish you represent.

Don't be alarmed by moments of silence. Sometimes ministers think they need to fill silences with conversation or action. There is nothing wrong with sitting in silence with another. In fact, these can be quite healing moments. God is present in the silence.

You should also be cognizant of those who are either not able to speak, have difficulty speaking, or speak rather slowly. Be patient and allow them to respond as they are able.

It is important that the extraordinary minister of Holy Communion keeps in mind the sacramental rites which are an essential part of the Church's ministry to the sick and dying and which can be administered only by an ordained bishop or priest—the Sacraments of Reconciliation and the Anointing of the Sick. As appropriate, it is part of your ministry to bring these to the attention of the sick and those confined to their homes, and if needed, to help them contact a priest.

Service to the People of God

Among these nuts and bolts of the ministry of care, never lose sight of your purpose. You have been commissioned in the name of Christ and his Church to serve as a bridge builder across the isolation that separates the sick and suffering from the parish community of faith and worship. Your deepest task is to carry the Good News of the Gospel to those who stand in need of its healing power. However, the most important tool is one that only Christ can provide for you. The more deeply you yourself enter into the heart of the Gospel message, the more clearly you will see that sick and healthy, young and old, grieving and rejoicing, struggling and at peace, are all one Body. In that Body, we are all servants of the Good News we proclaim, building one another up in faith and love until that day when, by God's gracious gift, we will all dwell together in the Lord's own house for ever and ever.

Genevieve Glen, OSB

Genevieve Glen, OSB, is a Benedictine nun of the contemplative Abbey of St. Walburga in Virginia Dale, Colorado. She holds master's degrees in systematic theology from Saint John's University, Collegeville, Minnesota, and in spirituality from the Catholic University of America in Washington DC, where she also did extensive doctoral studies in liturgy. She has lectured and written extensively on the Church's rites for the sick and dying.

About the Authors

Rev. Michael S. Driscoll, a priest of the Diocese of Helena, Montana, is associate professor emeritus of sacramental theology and liturgy at the University of Notre Dame. He is the founding director of of the graduate program in sacred music and the undergraduate minor in liturgical music at Notre Dame.

Rev. J. Philip Horrigan is the former director of the Department for Art and Architecture in the Office for Divine Worship for the Archdiocese of Chicago. He is a liturgical design consultant and is on the adjunct faculty for the Word and Worship Department at Catholic Theological Union in Chicago. His graduate degree in theology is from the Institute for Spirituality and Worship at the Jesuit School of Theology at Berkeley, and his doctorate of ministry in liturgical studies is from Catholic Theological Union in Chicago.

Rev. Keith McClellan, a priest of the Diocese of Gary, is the pastor of Notre Dame Parish, Michigan City, Indiana. He is a former Benedictine monk, and his ministries have included publishing, writing, leading retreats, and offering spiritual assistance.

Stephen S. Wilbricht, csc, a religious of the Congregation of Holy Cross, is an associate professor in the Department of Religious Studies and Theology at Stonehill College in Easton, Massachusetts. Prior to pursuing a doctorate in liturgical studies at the Catholic University of America in Washington, DC, he enjoyed seven years of pastoral ministry in two parishes in the Phoenix area, where he developed a love for Hispanic liturgy and culture. He has been a member of the North American Academy of Liturgy since 2011, participating in the work of the Christian Initiation Seminar and serving as its convener from 2015 to 2017.

The Rites

Orders for the Blessing of the Sick

INTRODUCTION

376 The blessing of the sick by the ministers of the Church is a very ancient custom, having its origins in the practice of Christ himself and his apostles. When ministers visit those who are sick, they are to respect the provisions of *Pastoral Care of the Sick: Rites of Anointing and Viaticum*, nos. 42–56, but the primary concern of every minister should be to show the sick how much Christ and his Church are concerned for them.

377 The text of *Pastoral Care of the Sick* indicates many occasions for blessing the sick and provides the blessing for formularies.[13]

378 The present order may be used by a priest or deacon. It may also be used by a layperson, who follows the rites and prayers designated for a lay minister. While maintaining the structure and chief elements of the rite, the minister should adapt the celebration to the circumstances of the place and the people involved.

379 When just one sick person is to be blessed, a priest or deacon may use the short formulary given in no. 406.

---

13. See Roman Ritual, Pastoral Care of the Sick: Rites of Anointing and Viaticum, no. 54.

Order of Blessing

A. Order for the Blessing of Adults
Introductory Rites

380   *When the community has gathered, the minister says:*

In the name of the Father, and of the Son, and of the Holy Spirit.

All make the sign of the cross and reply:

Amen.

382   *A lay minister greets those present in the following words.*

Brothers and sisters, let us bless the Lord, who went about doing good and healing the sick. Blessed be God now and for ever.

R. *Blessed be God now and for ever.*

Or:

R. *Amen.*

383   *In the following or similar words, the minister prepares the sick and all present for the blessing.*

The Lord Jesus, who went about doing good works and healing sickness and infirmity of every kind, commanded his disciples to care for the sick, to pray for them, and to lay hands on them. In this celebration we shall entrust our sick brothers and sisters to the care of the Lord, asking that he will enable them to bear their pain and suffering in the knowledge that, if they accept their share in the pain of his own passion, they will also share in its power to give comfort and strength.

Reading of the Word of God

384 A reader, another person present, or the minister reads a text of sacred Scripture, taken preferably from the texts given in Pastoral Care of the Sick *and the* Lectionary for Mass.[14] *The readings chosen should be those that best apply to the physical and spiritual condition of those who are sick.*

Brothers and sisters, listen to the words of the second letter of Paul to the Corinthians: 1:3–7

The God of all consolation.

Blessed be the God and Father of our Lord Jesus Christ, the Father of compassion and God of all encouragement, who encourages us in our every affliction, so that we may be able to encourage those who are in any affliction with the encouragement with which we ourselves are encouraged by God. For as Christ's sufferings overflow to us, so through Christ does our encouragement also overflow. If we are afflicted, it is for your encouragement and salvation; if we are encouraged, it is for your encouragement, which enables you to endure the same sufferings that we suffer. Our hope for you is firm, for we know that as you share in the sufferings, you also share in the encouragement.

385 *Or:*

Brothers and sisters, listen to the words of the holy gospel according to Matthew: 11:28–30

Come to me and I will refresh you.

Jesus said to the crowds: "Come to me, all you who labor and are burdened, and I will give you rest. Take my yoke upon you and learn from me, for I am meek and humble of heart;

---

14. See ibid, no. 297; Lectionary for Mass (2nd ed., 1981), nos. 790–795, 796–800 (Ritual Masses: V. Pastoral Care of the Sick and the Dying, 1. Anointing of the Sick and 2. Viaticum), and nos. 933–937 (Masses for Various Needs and Occasions, III. For Various Public Needs, 24. For the Sick).

and you will find rest for yourselves. For my yoke is easy, and my burden light."

386   Or:

**Brothers and sisters, listen to the words of
the holy gospel according to Mark:**   6:53–56
They laid the sick in the marketplace.

After making the crossing, Jesus and his disciples came to land at Gennesaret and tied up there. As they were leaving the boat, people immediately recognized him. They scurried about the surrounding country and began to bring in the sick on mats to wherever they heard he was. Whatever villages or towns or countryside he entered, they laid the sick in the marketplaces and begged him that they might touch only the tassel on his cloak; and as many as touched it were healed.

387   *As circumstances suggest, one of the following responsorial psalms may be sung or said, or some other suitable song.*

R. *Lord, you have preserved my life from destruction.*

Isaiah 38
Once I said,
"In the noontime of life I must depart!
To the gates of the nether world I shall be consigned
for the rest of my years." **R.**

I said, "I shall see the Lord no more
in the land of the living.
No longer shall I behold my fellow men
among those who dwell in the world." **R.**

My dwelling, like a shepherd's tent,
is struck down and borne away from me;
You have folded up my life, like a weaver
who severs the last thread. **R.**

Those live whom the LORD protects;
yours . . . the life of my spirit.
You have given me health and life. **R.**

Psalm 102:2–3, 24–25

R. *(v. 2) O Lord, hear my prayer, and let my cry come to you.*

388   As circumstances suggest, the minister may give those present a brief explanation of the biblical text, so that they may understand through faith the meaning of the celebration.

INTERCESSIONS

389   *The intercessions are then said. The minister introduces them and an assisting minister or one of those present announces the intentions. From the following intentions those best suited to the occasion may be used or adapted, or other intentions that apply to those who are sick and to the particular circumstances may be composed.*

The minister says:

The Lord Jesus loves our brothers and sisters who are ill.
With trust let us pray to him that he will comfort them with
his grace, saying:

R. *Lord, give those who are sick the comfort of your presence.*

Assisting minister:

Lord Jesus, you came as healer of body and of spirit, in order to cure all our ills. **R.**

Assisting minister:

You were a man of suffering, but it was our infirmities that you bore, our sufferings that you endured. **R.**

Assisting minister:

You chose to be like us in all things, in order to assure us of your compassion. **R.**

Assisting minister:

You experienced the weakness of the flesh in order to deliver us from evil. **R.**

Assisting minister:

At the foot of the cross your Mother stood as companion in your sufferings, and in your tender care you gave her to us as our Mother. **R.**

Assisting minister:

It is your wish that in our own flesh we should fill up what is wanting in your sufferings for the sake of your Body, the Church. **R.**

390 *Instead of the intercessions or in addition to them, one of the following litanies taken from Pastoral Care of the Sick, nos. 245 and 138 may be used.*

Minister:

You bore our weakness and carried our sorrows:
Lord, have mercy.

R. *Lord, have mercy.*

Minister:

You felt compassion for the crowd, and went about doing good and healing the sick: Christ, have mercy.

R. *Christ, have mercy.*

Minister:

You commanded your apostles to lay their hands on the sick in your name: Lord, have mercy.

R. *Lord, have mercy.*

391   Or:

The minister says:

Let us pray to God for our brothers and sisters and for all those who devote themselves to caring for them.

Assisting minister:

Bless **N.** and **N.** and fill them with new hope and strength: Lord, have mercy.

R. *Lord, have mercy.*

Assisting minister:

Relieve their pain: Lord, have mercy. **R.**

Assisting minister:

Free them from sin and do not let them give way to temptation: Lord, have mercy. **R.**

Assisting minister:

Sustain all the sick with your power: Lord, have mercy. **R.**

Assisting minister:

Assist all who care for the sick: Lord, have mercy. **R.**

Assisting minister:

Give life and health to our brothers and sisters on whom we lay our hands in your name: Lord, have mercy. **R.**

Prayer of Blessing

394   A lay minister traces the sign of the cross on the forehead of each sick person and says the following prayer of blessing.

Lord, our God,
who watch over your creatures with unfailing care,
keep us in the safe embrace of your love.
With your strong right hand raise up your servants
    (**N.** and **N.**)
and give them the strength of your own power.
Minister to them and heal their illnesses,
so that they may have from you the help they long for.

Through Christ our Lord.

R. *Amen.*

395   Or, for one sick person:

Lord and Father, almighty and eternal God,
by your blessing you give us strength and support
    in our frailty:
turn with kindness toward this your servant **N.**
Free him/her from all illness and restore him/her to health,
so that in the sure knowledge of your goodness
he/she will gratefully bless your holy name.

Through Christ our Lord.

R. *Amen.*

396   After the prayer of blessing the minister invites all present to pray for the protection of the Blessed Virgin. They may do so by singing or reciting a Marian antiphon, for example, We turn to you for protection (Sub tuum praesidium) *or* Hail, Holy Queen.

Concluding Rite

398   A lay minister invokes the Lord's blessing on the sick and all present by signing himself or herself with the sign of the cross and saying:

May the Lord Jesus Christ,
who went about doing good and healing the sick,
grant that we may have good health
and be enriched by his blessings.

R. Amen.

B. ORDER FOR THE BLESSING OF CHILDREN

399   For the blessing of sick children, the texts already given are to be adapted to the children's level, but special intercessions are provided here and a special prayer of blessing.

Intercessions

400   To the following intentions others may be added that apply to the condition of the sick children and to the particular circumstances.

The minister says:

The Lord Jesus loved and cherished the little ones with a special love. Let us, then, pray to him for these sick children, saying:

R. *Lord, keep them in all their ways.*

Or:

R. *Lord, hear our prayer.*

Assisting minister:

Lord Jesus, you called the little children to come to you and said that the kingdom of heaven belongs to such as these; listen with mercy to our prayers for these children. (For this we pray:) **R.**

Assisting minister:

You revealed the mysteries of the kingdom of heaven, not to the wise of this world, but to little children; give these children the proof of your love. (For this we pray:) **R.**

Assisting minister:

You praised the children who cried out their Hosannas on the eve of your Passion; strengthen these children and their parents with your holy comfort. (For this we pray:) **R.**

Assisting minister:

You charged your disciples to take care of the sick; stand at the side of all those who so gladly devote themselves to restoring the health of these children. (For this we pray:) **R.**

Prayer of Blessing

402   A lay minister, and particularly a mother or father when blessing a sick child, traces the sign of the cross on each child's forehead and then says the following prayer of blessing.

Father of mercy and God of all consolation,
you show tender care for all your creatures
and give health of soul and body.
Raise up these children
   (*or* this child *or* the son/daughter you have given us)
   from their (his/her) sickness.
Then, growing in wisdom and grace in your sight and ours,
they (he/she) will serve you all the days of their (his/her) life
in uprightness and holiness
and offer the thanksgiving due to your mercy.

Through Christ our Lord.

R. Amen.

C. SHORTER RITE

403 The minister says:

Our help is in the name of the Lord.

All reply:

Who made heaven and earth.

404 One of those present or the minister reads a text of sacred Scripture, for example:

2 Corinthians 1:3–4

Blessed be the God and Father of our Lord Jesus Christ, the Father of compassion and God of all encouragement, who encourages us in our every affliction, so that we may be able to encourage those who are in any affliction with the encouragement with which we ourselves are encouraged by God.

Matthew 11:28–29

Jesus said, "Come to me, all you who labor and are burdened, and I will give you rest. Take my yoke upon you and learn from me, for I am meek and humble of heart; and you will find rest for yourselves."

405 As circumstances suggest . . . a lay minister may trace the sign of the cross on the sick person's forehead while saying the prayer.

Lord and Father, almighty and eternal God,
by your blessing you give us strength and support
    in our frailty:
turn with kindness toward your servant, **N.**
Free him/her from all illness and restore him/her to health,
so that in the sure knowledge of your goodness
he/she will gratefully bless your holy name.

Through Christ our Lord.

R. Amen.

Order for the Blessing of a Person Suffering from Addiction or from Substance Abuse

INTRODUCTION

407   Addiction to alcohol, drugs, and other controlled substances causes great disruption in the life of an individual and his or her family. This blessing is intended to strengthen the addicted person in the struggle to overcome addiction and also to assist his or her family and friends.

408   This blessing may also be used for individuals who, although not addicted, abuse alcohol or drugs and wish the assistance of God's blessing in their struggle.

409   Ministers should be aware of the spiritual needs of a person suffering from addiction or substance abuse, and to this end the pastoral guidance on the care of the sick and rites of *Pastoral Care of the Sick* will be helpful.

410   If the recovery process is slow or is marked by relapses, the blessing may be repeated when pastorally appropriate.

411   These orders may be used by a priest or a deacon, and also by a layperson, who follows the rites and prayers designated for a lay minister.

A. ORDER OF BLESSING
INTRODUCTORY RITES

412 When the community has gathered, a suitable song may be sung. After the singing, the minister says:

In the name of the Father, and of the Son, and of the Holy Spirit.

All make the sign of the cross and reply:

Amen.

414 A lay minister greets those present in the following words:

Let us praise God our creator, who gives us courage and strength, now and for ever.

R. Amen.

415 In the following or similar words, the minister prepares those present for the blessing.

God created the world and all things in it and entrusted them into our hands that we might use them for our good and for the building up of the Church and human society. Today we pray for **N.**, that God may strengthen him/her in his/her weakness and restore him/her to the freedom of God's children. We pray also for ourselves that we may encourage and support him/her in the days ahead.

Reading of the Word of God

416   A reader, another person present, or the minister reads a text of sacred Scripture.

Brothers and sisters, listen to the words of the second letter of Paul to the Corinthians: 4:6–9

We are afflicted, but not crushed.

For God who said, "Let light shine out of darkness," has shone in our hearts to bring to light the knowledge of the glory of God on the face of Jesus Christ.

But we hold this treasure in earthen vessels, that the surpassing power may be of God and not from us. We are afflicted in every way, but not constrained; perplexed, but not driven to despair; persecuted, but not abandoned; struck down, but not destroyed.

417   Or:

Isaiah 63:7-9—He has favored us according to his mercy.

Romans 8:18-25—I consider the sufferings of the present to be as nothing compared with the glory to be revealed in us.

Matthew 15:21-28—Woman, you have great faith.

418   As circumstances suggest, one of the following responsorial psalms may be sung or said, or some other suitable song.

R. *Our help is from the Lord who made heaven and earth.*

Psalm 121
I lift up my eyes toward the mountains;
whence shall help come to me?
My help is from the Lord
who made heaven and earth. **R.**

May he not suffer your foot to slip;
may he slumber not who guards you:
Indeed he neither slumbers nor sleeps,
the guardian of Israel. **R.**

The Lord is your guardian; the Lord is your shade;
he is beside you at your right hand.
The sun shall not harm you by day,
nor the moon by night. **R.**

The Lord will guard you from all evil;
he will guard your life.
The Lord will guard your coming and your going,
both now and forever. **R.**

Psalm 130:1-2, 3-4, 5-6, 7-8

R. *(v. 5) My soul trusts in the Lord.*

419   *As circumstances suggest, the minister may give those present a brief explanation of the biblical text, so that they may understand through faith the meaning of the celebration.*

INTERCESSIONS

420   *The intercessions are then said. The minister introduces them and an assisting minister or one of those present announces the intentions. From the following those best suited to the occasion may be used or adapted, or other intentions that apply to the particular circumstances may be composed.*

The minister says:

Our God gives us life and constantly calls us to new life; let us pray to God with confidence.

R. *Lord, hear our prayer.*

Assisting minister:

For those addicted to alcohol/drugs, that God may be their strength and support, we pray. **R.**

Assisting minister:

For **N.**, bound by the chains of addiction/substance abuse, that we encourage and assist him/her in his/her struggle, we pray. **R.**

Assisting minister:

For **N.**, that he/she may trust in the mercy of God through whom all things are possible, we pray. **R.**

Assisting minister:

For the family and friends of **N.**, that with faith and patience they show him/her their love, we pray. **R.**

Assisting minister:

For the Church, that it may always be attentive to those in need, we pray. **R.**

421   *After the intercessions the minister, in the following or similar words, invites all present to sing or say the Lord's Prayer.*

Let us pray to our merciful God as Jesus taught us:

All:

Our Father . . .

Prayer of Blessing

422   *A lay minister says the prayer with hands joined.*

A   *For addiction*

God of mercy,
we bless you in the name of your Son, Jesus Christ,
who ministered to all who came to him.
Give your strength to **N.,** your servant,
bound by the chains of addiction.
Enfold him/her in your love
and restore him/her to the freedom of God's children.

Lord,
look with compassion on all those
who have lost their health and freedom.
Restore to them the assurance of your unfailing mercy,
and strengthen them in the work of recovery.

To those who care for them,
grant patient understanding and a love that perseveres.

Through Christ our Lord.
R. *Amen.*

B   *For substance abuse*

God of mercy,
we bless you in the name of your Son, Jesus Christ,
who ministered to all who came to him.
Give your strength to **N.,** your servant,
enfold him/her in your love
and restore him/her to the freedom of God's children.

Lord,
look with compassion on all those
who have lost their health and freedom.
Restore to them the assurance of your unfailing mercy,
strengthen them in the work of recovery,
and help them to resist all temptation.

To those who care for them,
grant patient understanding and a love that perseveres.

Through Christ our Lord.

R. *Amen.*

As circumstances suggest, the minister in silence may sprinkle the person with holy water.

Concluding Rite

424   *A lay minister concludes the rite by signing himself or herself with the sign of the cross and saying:*

May our all-merciful God, Father, Son, and Holy Spirit, bless us and embrace us in love for ever.

R. *Amen.*

425   *It is preferable to end the celebration with a suitable song.*

B. SHORTER RITE

426   *All make the sign of the cross as the minister says:*

Our help is in the name of the Lord.

All reply:

Who made heaven and earth.

427   One of those present or the minister reads a text of sacred Scripture, for example:

Brothers and sisters, listen to the words of the second letter of Paul to the Corinthians: 4:6–9

We are afflicted, but not crushed.

For God who said, "Let light shine out of darkness," has shone in our hearts to bring to light the knowledge of the glory of God on the face of Jesus Christ.

But we hold this treasure in earthen vessels, that the surpassing power may be of God and not from us. We are afflicted in every way, but not constrained; perplexed, but not driven to despair; persecuted, but not abandoned; struck down, but not destroyed.

428   Or:
Isaiah 63:7-9—He has favored us according to his mercy.
Matthew 15:21-28—Woman, you have great faith.

429   A lay minister says the prayer with hands joined.

A   *For addiction*

God of mercy,
we bless you in the name of your Son, Jesus Christ,
who ministered to all who came to him.
Give your strength to **N.**, your servant,
bound by the chains of addiction.
Enfold him/her in your love
and restore him/her to the freedom of God's children.

Lord,
look with compassion on all those
who have lost their health and freedom.
Restore to them the assurance of your unfailing mercy,
and strengthen them in the work of recovery.

To those who care for them,
grant patient understanding and a love that perseveres.

Through Christ our Lord.
R. *Amen.*

B   *For substance abuse*

God of mercy,
we bless you in the name of your Son, Jesus Christ,
who ministered to all who came to him.
Give your strength to *N.*, your servant,
enfold him/her in your love
and restore him/her to the freedom of God's children.

Lord,
look with compassion on all those
who have lost their health and freedom.
Restore to them the assurance of your unfailing mercy,
strengthen them in the work of recovery,
and help them to resist all temptation.

To those who care for them,
grant patient understanding and a love that perseveres.

Through Christ our Lord.
R. *Amen.*

Order for the Blessing of a Victim of Crime or Oppression

INTRODUCTION

430   The personal experience of a crime, political oppression, or social oppression can be traumatic and not easily forgotten. A victim often needs the assistance of others, and no less that of God, in dealing with this experience.

431   This blessing is intended to assist the victim and help him or her come to a state of tranquility and peace.

432   These orders may be used by a priest or a deacon, and also by a layperson, who follows the rites and prayers designated for a lay minister.

A. ORDER OF BLESSING

INTRODUCTORY RITES

433   When the community has gathered, a suitable song may be sung. After the singing, the minister says:

In the name of the Father, and of the Son, and of the Holy Spirit.

All make the sign of the cross and reply:

Amen.

435   A lay minister greets those present in the following words:

May the Lord grant us peace, now and for ever.

R. Amen.

436   In the following or similar words, the minister prepares those present for the blessing.

Throughout history God has manifested his love and care for those who have suffered from violence, hatred, and oppression. We commend **N.** to the healing mercy of God who binds up all our wounds and enfolds us in his gentle care.

READING OF THE WORD OF GOD

437   A reader, another person present, or the minister reads a text of sacred Scripture.

Brothers and sisters, listen to the words of the holy gospel according to Matthew: 10:28–33

Do not fear.

Jesus said to his disciples: "Do not be afraid of those who kill the body but cannot kill the soul; rather, be afraid of the one who can destroy both soul and body in Gehenna. Are not two sparrows sold for a small coin? Yet not one of them falls to the ground without your Father's knowledge. Even all the hairs of your head are counted. So do not be afraid; you are worth more than many sparrows. Everyone who acknowledges me before others I will acknowledge before my heavenly Father. But whoever denies me before others, I will deny before my heavenly Father."

438   Or:

Isaiah 59:6b-8, 15-18—The Lord is appalled by evil and injustice.

Job 3:1-26—Lamentation of Job.

Lamentations 3:1-24—I am one who knows affliction.

Lamentations 3:49-59—When I called, you came to my aid.

Micah 4:1-4—Every person shall sit undisturbed.

Matthew 5:1-10—The beatitudes.

Matthew 5:43-48—Love your enemies, pray for those who persecute you.

Luke 10:25-37—The good Samaritan.

439   As circumstances suggest, one of the following responsorial psalms may be sung, or some other suitable song.

R. The Lord is my strength and my salvation.

Psalm 140

Deliver me, O Lord, from evil men;
preserve me from violent men,
From those who devise evil in their hearts,
and stir up wars every day. **R.**

Save me, O Lord, from the hands of the wicked;
preserve me from violent men
Who plan to trip up my feet—
the proud who have hidden a trap for me;
They have spread cords for a net;
by the wayside they have laid snares for me. **R.**

Grant not, O L{ORD}, the desires of the wicked;
further not their plans.
Those who surround me lift up their heads;
may the mischief which they threaten overwhelm them. **R.**

I know that the L{ORD} renders
justice to the afflicted, judgment to the poor.
Surely the just shall give thanks to your name;
the upright shall dwell in your presence. **R.**

Psalm 142:2–3, 4b–5, 6–7
***R.** (v. 6) You, O Lord, are my refuge.*

Psalm 31:2–3a, 4–5, 15–16, 24–25
***R.** (v. 6) Into your hands I commend my spirit.*

440   As circumstances suggest, the minister may give those present a brief explanation of the biblical text, so that they may understand through faith the meaning of the celebration.

INTERCESSIONS

441   The intercessions are then said. The minister introduces them and an assisting minister or one of those present announces the intentions. From the following those best suited to the occasion may be used or adapted, or other intentions that apply to the particular circumstances may be composed.

The minister says:
Let us pray to the Lord God, the defender of the
weak and powerless, who delivered our ancestors from harm.

R. *Deliver us from evil, O Lord.*

Assisting minister:

For **N.**, that he/she may be freed from pain and fear, we pray to the Lord. **R.**

Assisting minister:

For all who are victims of crime/oppression, we pray to the Lord. **R.**

Assisting minister:

For an end to all acts of violence and hatred, we pray to the Lord. **R.**

Assisting minister:

For those who harm others, that they may change their lives and turn to God, we pray to the Lord. **R.**

442   *After the intercessions the minister, in the following or similar words, invites all present to sing or say the Lord's Prayer.*

The Lord heals our wounds and strengthens us in our weakness; let us pray as Christ has taught us:
All:

Our Father . . .

Prayer of Blessing

443   A lay minister says the prayer with hands joined.

Lord God,
your own Son was delivered into the hands of the wicked,
yet he prayed for his persecutors
and overcame hatred with the blood of the cross.
Relieve the suffering of **N.**;
grant him/her peace of mind
and a renewed faith in your protection and care.

Protect us all from the violence of others,
keep us safe from the weapons of hate,
and restore to us tranquility and peace.

Through Christ our Lord.
R. Amen.

As circumstances suggest, the minister in silence may sprinkle the person with holy water.

Concluding Rite

445   A lay minister concludes the rite by signing himself or herself with the Sign of the Cross and saying:

May God bless us with his mercy,
strengthen us with his love,
and enable us to walk in charity and peace.

R. Amen.

446   It is preferable to end the celebration with a suitable song.

B. SHORTER RITE

447   All make the sign of the cross as the minister says:

Our help is in the name of the Lord.

All reply:
Who made heaven and earth.

448   One of those present or the minister reads a text of sacred Scripture, for example:

Brothers and sisters, listen to the words of the holy gospel according to Matthew: 10:28–33

Do not fear.

Jesus said to his disciples: "Do not be afraid of those who kill the body but cannot kill the soul; rather, be afraid of the one who can destroy both soul and body in Gehenna. Are not two sparrows sold for a small coin? Yet not one of them falls to the ground without your Father's knowledge. Even all the hairs of your head are counted. So do not be afraid; you are worth more than many sparrows. Everyone who acknowledges me before others I will acknowledge before my heavenly Father. But whoever denies me before others, I will deny before my heavenly Father."

449   Or:
Isaiah 59:6b–8, 15–18—The Lord is appalled by evil and injustice.
Job 3:1–26—Lamentation of Job.
Lamentations 3:1–24—I am a man who knows affliction.
Lamentations 3:49–59—When I called, you came to my aid.
Matthew 5:1–10—The beatitudes.
Luke 10:25–37—The good Samaritan.

450   A lay minister says the prayer with hands joined.

Lord God,
your own Son was delivered into the hands of the wicked
yet he prayed for his persecutors
and overcame hatred with the blood of the cross.
Relieve the suffering of **N.**;
grant him/her peace of mind
and a renewed faith in your protection and care.

Protect us all from the violence of others,
keep us safe from the weapons of hate,
and restore to us tranquility and peace.

Through Christ our Lord.

R. *Amen.*

Order for the Blessing of Parents after a Miscarriage

INTRODUCTION

279   In times of death and grief the Christian turns to the Lord for consolation and strength. This is especially true when a child dies before birth. This blessing is provided to assist the parents in their grief and console them with the blessing of God.

280   The minister should be attentive to the needs of the parents and other family members and to this end the introduction to the *Order of Christian Funerals,* Part II: Funeral Rites for Children will be helpful.

281   These orders may be used by a priest or deacon, and also by a layperson who follows the rites and prayers designated for a lay minister.

A. ORDER OF BLESSING
INTRODUCTORY RITES

282 When the community has gathered, a suitable song may be sung. The minister says:

In the name of the Father, and of the Son, and of the Holy Spirit.

All make the sign of the cross and reply:

Amen.

284 A lay minister greets those present in the following words:

Let us praise the Father of mercies, the God of all consolation. Blessed be God for ever.

R. *Blessed be God for ever.*

285 In the following or similar words, the minister prepares those present for the blessing.

For those who trust in God,
in the pain of sorrow there is consolation,
in the face of despair there is hope,
in the midst of death there is life.
N. and N., as we mourn the death of your child
we place ourselves in the hands of God
and ask for strength, for healing, and for love.

READING OF THE WORD OF GOD

286 A reader, another person present, or the minister reads a text of sacred Scripture.

Brothers and sisters, listen to the words of the book of Lamentations: 3:17–26

Hope in the Lord.
My soul is deprived of peace,
I have forgotten what happiness is;
I tell myself my future is lost,
all that I hoped for from the LORD.
The thought of my homeless poverty
is wormwood and gall;
Remembering it over and over
leaves my soul downcast within me.
But I will call this to mind,
as my reason to have hope:
The favors of the LORD are not exhausted,
his mercies are not spent;
They are renewed each morning,
so great is his faithfulness.
My portion is the LORD, says my soul;
therefore will I hope in him.
Good is the LORD to one who waits for him,
to the soul that seeks him;
It is good to hope in silence
for the saving help of the LORD.

287   Or:

Isaiah 49:8–13—In a time of favor I answer you, on the day of salvation I help you.

Romans 8:18–27—In hope we were saved.

Romans 8:26–31—If God is for us, who can be against us?

Colossians 1:9–12—We have been praying for you unceasingly.

Hebrews 5:7–10—Christ intercedes for us.

Luke 22:39–46—Agony in the garden.

288   *As circumstances suggest, one of the following responsorial psalms may be sung, or some other suitable song.*

R. *To you, O Lord, I lift up my soul.*

Psalm 25

Your ways, O Lord, make known to me;
teach me your paths,
Guide me in your truth and teach me,
for you are God my savior,
and for you I wait all the day. **R.**

Remember that your compassion, O Lord,
and your kindness are from of old.
The sins of my youth and my frailties remember not;
in your kindness remember me
because of your goodness, O Lord. **R.**

Look toward me, and have pity on me,
for I am alone and afflicted.
Relieve the troubles of my heart,
and bring me out of my distress. **R.**

Preserve my life, and rescue me;
let me not be put to shame, for I take refuge in you.
Let integrity and uprightness preserve me,
because I wait for you, O Lord. **R.**

Psalm 143:1, 5–6, 8, 10

R. *(v. 1) O Lord, hear my prayer.*

289 *As circumstances suggest, the minister may give those present a brief explanation of the biblical text, so that they may understand through faith the meaning of the celebration.*

INTERCESSIONS

290 *The intercessions are then said. The minister introduces them and an assisting minister or one of those present announces the intentions. From the following those best suited to the occasion may be used or adapted, or other intentions that apply to the particular circumstances may be composed.*

The minister says:

Let us pray to God who throughout the ages has heard the cries of parents.

R. *Lord, hear our prayer.*

Assisting minister:

For **N.** and **N.**, who know the pain of grief, that they may be comforted, we pray. **R.**

Assisting minister:

For this family, that it may find new hope in the midst of suffering, we pray. **R.**

Assisting minister:

For these parents, that they may learn from the example of Mary, who grieved by the cross of her Son, we pray. **R.**

Assisting minister:

For all who have suffered the loss of a child, that Christ may be their support, we pray. **R.**

291   *After the intercessions the minister, in the following or similar words, invites all present to sing or say the Lord's Prayer.*

Let us pray to the God of consolation and hope, as Christ has taught us:

All:

Our Father . . .

Prayer of Blessing

292   *A lay minister says the prayer with hands joined.*

Compassionate God,
soothe the hearts of **N.** and **N.**,
and grant that through the prayers of Mary,
who grieved by the cross of her Son,
you may enlighten their faith,
give hope to their hearts,
and peace to their lives.

Lord,
grant mercy to all the members of this family
and comfort them with the hope
that one day we will all live with you,
with your Son Jesus Christ, and the Holy Spirit,
for ever and ever.
R. *Amen.*

293   Or:

Lord,
God of all creation
we bless and thank you for your tender care.
Receive this life you created in love
and comfort your faithful people in their time of loss
with the assurance of your unfailing mercy.

Through Christ our Lord.

R. *Amen.*

As circumstances suggest, the minister in silence may sprinkle the parents with holy water.

Concluding Rite

295   A lay minister concludes the rite by signing himself or herself with the sign of the cross and saying:

May God give us peace in our sorrow,
consolation in our grief,
and strength to accept his will in all things.

R. *Amen.*

296   It is preferable to end the celebration with a suitable song.

B. SHORTER RITE

297   All make the sign of the cross as the minister says:

Our help is in the name of the Lord.

All reply:
Who made heaven and earth.

298   One of those present or the minister reads a text of sacred Scripture, for example:

Brothers and sisters, listen to the words of the book of Lamentations: 3:17–26

Hope in the Lord.

My soul is deprived of peace,
I have forgotten what happiness is;
I tell myself my future is lost,
all that I hoped for from the Lord.
The thought of my homeless poverty
is wormwood and gall;
Remembering it over and over
leaves my soul downcast within me.
But I will call this to mind,
as my reason to have hope:
The favors of the Lord are not exhausted,
his mercies are not spent;
They are renewed each morning,
so great is his faithfulness.
My portion is the Lord, says my soul;
therefore will I hope in him.
Good is the Lord to one who waits for him,
to the soul that seeks him;
It is good to hope in silence
for the saving help of the Lord.

299 Or:

Romans 8:26–31—If God is for us, who can be against us?
Colossians 1:9–12—We have been praying for you unceasingly.

300 *A lay minister says the prayer with hands joined.*

Compassionate God,
soothe the hearts of **N.** and **N.**,
and grant that through the prayers of Mary,
who grieved by the cross of her Son,
you may enlighten their faith,
give hope to their hearts,
and peace to their lives.

Lord,
grant mercy to all the members of this family
and comfort them with the hope
that one day we will all live with you,
with your Son Jesus Christ, and the Holy Spirit,
for ever and ever.

R. Amen.

301 Or:

Lord,
God of all creation,
we bless and thank you for your tender care.
Receive this life you created in love
and comfort your faithful people in their time of loss
with the assurance of your unfailing mercy.

Through Christ our Lord.
R. Amen.

Pastoral Care of the Sick

INTRODUCTION

Lord, your friend is sick.

42   The rites in Part I of *Pastoral Care of the Sick: Rites of Anointing and Viaticum* are used by the Church to comfort the sick in time of anxiety, to encourage them to fight against illness, and perhaps to restore them to health. These rites are distinct from those in the second part of this book, which are provided to comfort and strengthen a Christian in the passage from this life.

43   The concern that Christ showed for the bodily and spiritual welfare of those who are ill is continued by the Church in its ministry to the sick. This ministry is the common responsibility of all Christians, who should visit the sick, remember them in prayer, and celebrate the sacraments with them. The family and friends of the sick, doctors and others who care for them, and Priests with pastoral responsibilities have a particular share in this ministry of comfort. Through words of encouragement and faith they can help the sick to unite themselves with the sufferings of Christ for the good of God's people.

    Remembrance of the sick is especially appropriate at common worship on the Lord's Day, during the Universal Prayer at Mass and in the intercessions at Morning Prayer and Evening Prayer. Family members and those who are dedicated to the care of the sick should be remembered on these occasions as well.

44   Priests have the special task of preparing the sick to celebrate the Sacrament of Penance (individually or in a communal celebration), to receive the Eucharist frequently if their condition permits, and to celebrate the Sacrament of Anointing at the appropriate time. During this preparation it will be especially helpful if the sick person, the Priest, and the family become accustomed to praying together. The Priest should provide leadership to those who assist him in the care of the sick, especially Deacons and other ministers of the Eucharist.

The words "Priest," "Deacon," and "minister" are used advisedly. Only in those rites which must be celebrated by a Priest is the word "Priest" used in the rubrics (that is, the Sacrament of Penance, the Sacrament of the Anointing of the Sick, the celebration of Viaticum within Mass). Whenever it is clear that, in the absence of a Priest, a Deacon may preside at a particular rite, the words "Priest or Deacon" are used in the rubrics. Whenever another minister is permitted to celebrate a rite in the absence of a Priest or Deacon, the word "minister" is used in the rubrics, even though in many cases the rite will be celebrated by a Priest or Deacon.

45   The pastoral care of the sick should be suited to the nature and length of the illness. An illness of short duration in which the full recovery of health is a possibility requires a more intensive ministry, whereas illness of a longer duration which may be a prelude to death requires a more extensive ministry. An awareness of the attitudes and emotional states which these different situations engender in the sick is indispensable to the development of an appropriate ministry.

Visits to the Sick

46   Those who visit the sick should help them to pray, sharing with them the word of God proclaimed in the assembly from which their sickness has separated them. As the occasion permits, prayer drawn from the psalms or from other prayers or litanies may be added to the word of God. Care should be taken to prepare for a future visit during which the sick will receive the Eucharist.

Visits to a Sick Child

47   What has already been said about visiting the sick and praying with them (see no. 46) applies also in visits to a sick child. Every effort should be made to know the child and to accommodate the care in keeping with the age and comprehension of the child. In these circumstances the minister should also be particularly concerned to help the child's family.

48   If it is appropriate, the Priest may discuss with the parents the possibility of preparing and celebrating with the child the Sacraments of Initiation (Baptism, Confirmation, Eucharist). The Priest may baptize and confirm the child (see *Rite of Confirmation,* no. 7b). To complete the process of Initiation, the child should also receive first Communion. (If the child is a proper subject for Confirmation, then he or she may receive first Communion in accordance with the practice of the Church.) There is no reason to delay this, especially if the illness is likely to be a long one.

49   Throughout the illness the minister should ensure that the child receives Communion frequently, making whatever adaptations seem necessary in the rite for Communion of the sick (Chapter III).

50   The child is to be anointed if he or she has sufficient use of reason to be strengthened by the Sacrament of Anointing. The rites provided (Chapter IV) are to be used and adapted.

Communion of the Sick

51   Because the sick are prevented from celebrating the Eucharist with the rest of the community, the most important visits are those during which they receive Holy Communion. In receiving the Body and Blood of Christ, the sick are united sacramentally to the Lord and are reunited with the Eucharistic community from which illness has separated them.

Anointing of the Sick

52   The Priest should be especially concerned for those whose health has been seriously impaired by illness or old age. He will offer them a new sign of hope: the laying on of hands and the Anointing of the Sick accompanied by the prayer of faith (James 5:14). Those who receive this sacrament in the faith of the Church will find it a true sign of comfort and support in time of trial. It will work to overcome the sickness, if this is God's will.

53   Some types of mental sickness are now classified as serious. Those who are judged to have a serious mental illness and who would be strengthened by the sacrament may be anointed (see no. 5). The anointing may be repeated in accordance with the conditions for other kinds of serious illness (see no. 9).

Visits to the Sick

INTRODUCTION

I was sick, and you visited me.

54   The prayers contained in this chapter follow the common pattern of reading, response, prayer, and blessing. This pattern is provided as an example of what can be done and may be adapted as necessary. The minister may wish to invite those present to prepare for the reading from Scripture, perhaps by a brief introduction or through a moment of silence. The laying on of hands may be added by the Priest, if appropriate, after the blessing is given.

55   The sick should be encouraged to pray when they are alone or with their families, friends, or those who care for them. Their prayer should be drawn primarily from Scripture. The sick person and others may help to plan the celebration, for example, by choosing the prayers and readings. Those making these choices should keep in mind the condition of the sick person.

The passages found in this chapter and those included in Part III speak of the mystery of human suffering in the words, works, and life of Christ. Occasionally, for example, on the Lord's Day, the sick may feel more involved in the worship of the community from which they are separated if the readings used are those assigned for that day in the Lectionary. Prayers may also be drawn from the psalms or from other prayers or litanies. The sick should be helped in making this form of prayer, and the minister should always be ready to pray with them.

56   The minister should encourage the sick person to offer his or her sufferings in union with Christ and to join in prayer for the Church and the world. Some examples of particular intentions which may be suggested to the sick person are: for peace in the world; for a deepening of the life of the Spirit in the local Church; for the pope and the bishops; for people suffering in a particular disaster.

READING

57   *The word of God is proclaimed by one of those present or by the minister. An appropriate reading from Part III or one of the following readings may be used:*

A   *Acts of the Apostles 3:1–10*

In the name of Jesus and the power of his Church, there is salvation—even liberation from sickness.

B   *Matthew 8:14–17*

Jesus fulfills the prophetic figure of the servant of God taking upon himself and relieving the sufferings of God's people.

RESPONSE

58   *A brief period of silence may be observed after the reading of the word of God. An appropriate psalm from Part III or one of the following psalms may be used:*

A   *Psalm 102*

R. *O Lord, hear my prayer and let my cry come to you.*

O Lord, hear my prayer,
  and let my cry come to you.
Hide not your face from me
  in the day of my distress.
Incline your ear to me;
  in the day when I call, answer me speedily. **R.**

He has broken down my strength in the way;
   he has cut short my days. I say: O my God,
Take me not hence in the midst of my days;
   through all generations your years endure. **R.**

Of old you established the earth,
   and the heavens are the work of your hands.
They shall perish, but you remain
   though all of them grow old like a garment.
Like clothing you change them, and they are changed,
   but you are the same, and your years have no end. **R.**

Let this be written for the generation to come,
   and let his future creatures praise the LORD:
"The LORD looked down from his holy height,
   from heaven he beheld the earth,
To hear the groaning of the prisoners,
   to release those doomed to die." **R.**

B   *Psalm 27*

R. *The Lord is my light and my salvation.*

The LORD is my light and my salvation;
   whom should I fear?
The LORD is my life's refuge;
   of whom should I be afraid? **R.**

One thing I ask of the LORD;
   this I seek:
To dwell in the house of the LORD
   all the days of my life
That I may gaze on the loveliness of the LORD
   and contemplate his temple. **R.**

For he will hide me in his abode
   in the day of trouble,
He will conceal me in the shelter of his tent,
   he will set me high upon a rock. **R.**

The minister may then give a brief explanation of the reading, applying it to the needs of the sick person and those who are looking after him or her.

THE LORD'S PRAYER

59   *The minister introduces the Lord's Prayer in these or similar words:*

Now let us offer together the prayer our Lord Jesus Christ taught us:

All say:
Our Father . . .

CONCLUDING PRAYER

60   *The minister says a concluding prayer. One of the following may be used:*

A

O God, who willed that our infirmities
be borne by your Only Begotten Son
to show the value of human suffering,
listen in kindness to our prayers
for our brothers and sisters who are sick;
grant that all who are oppressed by pain, distress
      or other afflictions

may know that they are chosen
among those proclaimed blessed
and are united to Christ
in his suffering for the salvation of the world.
Through Christ our Lord.

R. Amen.

B

Almighty ever-living God, eternal health of believers,
hear our prayers for your servants who are sick:
grant them, we implore you, your merciful help,
so that, with their health restored,
they may give you thanks in the midst of your Church.
Through Christ our Lord.

R. Amen.

C

All-powerful and ever-living God,
we find security in your forgiveness.
Give us serenity and peace of mind;
may we rejoice in your gifts of kindness
and use them always for your glory and our good.

We ask this in the name of Jesus the Lord.

R. Amen.

BLESSING

61   *The minister may give a blessing. One of the following may be used:*

A

All praise and glory is yours, Lord our God,
for you have called us to serve you in love.
Bless **N.**
so that he/she may bear this illness
in union with your Son's obedient suffering.
Restore him/her to health,
and lead him/her to glory.

Through Christ our Lord.
R. *Amen.*

B

For an elderly person

All praise and glory are yours, Lord our God,
for you have called us to serve you in love.
Bless all who have grown old in your service
and give **N.** strength and courage
to continue to follow Jesus your Son.

Through Christ our Lord.
R. *Amen.*

A minister who is not a Priest or Deacon invokes God's blessing and makes the Sign of the Cross on himself or herself, while saying:

May the Lord bless us,
protect us from all evil,
and bring us to everlasting life.

R. *Amen.*

The minister may then trace the Sign of the Cross on the sick person's forehead.

Visits to a Sick Child

INTRODUCTION

Let the children come to me; do not keep them back from me.

62	The following readings, prayers, and blessings will help the minister to pray with sick children and their families. They are provided as an example of what can be done and may be adapted as necessary. The minister may wish to invite those present to prepare for the reading from Scripture, perhaps by a brief introduction or through a moment of silence.

63	If the child does not already know the minister, the latter should seek to establish a friendly and easy relationship with the child. Therefore, the greeting which begins the visit should be an informal one.

64	The minister should help sick children to understand that the sick are very special in the eyes of God because they are suffering as Christ suffered and because they can offer their sufferings for the salvation of the world.

65	In praying with the sick child the minister chooses, together with the child and the family if possible, suitable elements of common prayer in the form of a brief Liturgy of the Word. This may consist of a reading from Scripture, simple one-line prayers taken from Scripture which can be repeated by the child, other familiar prayers such as the Lord's Prayer, the Hail Mary, litanies, or a simple form of the Universal Prayer. The laying on of hands may be added by the Priest, if appropriate, after the child has been blessed.

READING

66   One of the following readings may be used for a brief Liturgy of the Word. Other readings may be chosen, for example: Mark 5:21-23, 35-43, Jesus raises the daughter of Jairus and gives her back to her parents; Mark 9:14-27, Jesus cures a boy and gives him back to his father; Luke 7:11-15, Jesus raises a young man, the only son of his mother, and gives him back to her; John 4:46-53, Jesus gives his second sign by healing an official's son. In addition, other stories concerning the Lord's healing ministry may be found suitable, especially if told with the simplicity and clarity of one of the children's versions of Scripture.

A   *Mark 9:33-37*

Jesus proposes the child as the ideal of those who would enter the kingdom.

B   *Mark 10:13-16*

Jesus welcomes the children and lays hands on them.

RESPONSE

67   After the reading of the word of God, time may be set apart for silent reflection if the child is capable of this form of prayer. The minister should also explain the meaning of the reading to those present, adapting it to their circumstances.

The minister may then help the child and the family to respond to the word of God. The following short responsory may be used:

Jesus, come to me.

—*Jesus, come to me.*

Jesus, put your hand on me.

—*Jesus, put your hand on me.*

Jesus, bless me.

—*Jesus, bless me.*

The Lord's Prayer

68   *The minister introduces the Lord's Prayer in these or similar words:*

Let us pray to the Father using those words which Jesus himself used:

All say:

Our Father . . .

Concluding Prayer

69   *The minister says a concluding prayer. One of the following may be used.*

A

God of love,
ever caring,
ever strong,
stand by us in our time of need.

Watch over your child **N.** who is sick,
look after him/her in every danger,
and grant him/her your healing and peace.

We ask this in the name of Jesus the Lord.
R. Amen.

B

Father,
in your love
you gave us Jesus
to help us rise triumphant over grief and pain.

Look on your child **N.** who is sick
and see in his/her sufferings those of your Son.

Grant **N.** a share in the strength you granted your Son
that he/she too may be a sign
of your goodness, kindness, and loving care.

We ask this in the name of Jesus the Lord.
R. *Amen.*

BLESSING

70   *The minister makes a Sign of the Cross on the child's forehead, saying one of the following:*

A

N., when you were baptized,
you were marked with the Cross of Jesus.
I (we) make this cross ✠ on your forehead
and ask the Lord to bless you,
and restore you to health.

R. *Amen.*

B

All praise and glory is yours, heavenly God,
for you have called us to serve you in love.
Have mercy on us and listen to our prayer
as we ask you to help **N.**

Bless ✠ your beloved child,
and restore him/her to health
in the name of Jesus the Lord.

R. Amen.

Each one present may in turn trace the Sign of the Cross on the child's forehead, in silence.

A minister who is not a Priest or Deacon invokes God's blessing and makes the Sign of the Cross on himself or herself, while saying:

May the Lord bless us,
protect us from all evil,
and bring us to everlasting life.

R. Amen.

Communion of the Sick

INTRODUCTION

Whoever eats this bread will live for ever.

71   This chapter contains two rites: one for use when Communion can be celebrated in the context of a Liturgy of the Word; the other, a brief Communion rite for use in more restrictive circumstances, such as in hospitals.

72   Priests with pastoral responsibilities should see to it that the sick or aged, even though not seriously ill or in danger of death, are given every opportunity to receive the Eucharist frequently, even daily, especially during Easter Time. They may receive Communion at any hour. Those who care for the sick may receive Communion with them, in accord with the usual norms. To provide frequent Communion for the sick, it may be necessary to ensure that the community has a sufficient number of Extraordinary Ministers of Holy Communion. The minister should wear attire appropriate to this ministry.

   The sick person and others may help to plan the celebration, for example, by choosing the prayers and readings. Those making these choices should keep in mind the condition of the sick person. The readings should help those present to reach a deeper understanding of the mystery of human suffering in relation to the Paschal Mystery of Christ.

73   The faithful who are ill are deprived of their rightful and accustomed place in the Eucharistic community. In bringing Communion to them the Extraordinary Minister of Holy Communion represents Christ and manifests faith and charity on behalf of the whole community toward those who cannot be present at the Eucharist. For the sick the reception of Communion is not only a privilege but also a sign of support and concern shown by the Christian community for its members who are ill.

The links between the community's Eucharistic celebration, especially on the Lord's Day, and the Communion of the sick are intimate and manifold. Besides remembering the sick in the Universal Prayer at Mass, those present should be reminded occasionally of the significance of Communion in the lives of those who are ill: union with Christ in his struggle with evil, his prayer for the world, and his love for the Father, and union with the community from which they are separated.

The obligation to visit and comfort those who cannot take part in the Eucharistic assembly may be clearly demonstrated by taking Communion to them from the community's Eucharistic celebration. This symbol of unity between the community and its sick members has the deepest significance on the Lord's Day, the special day of the Eucharistic assembly.

74   When the Eucharist is brought to the sick, it should be carried in a pyx or small closed container. Those who are with the sick should be asked to prepare a table covered with a linen cloth upon which the Blessed Sacrament will be placed. Lighted candles are prepared and, where it is customary, a vessel of holy water. Care should be taken to make the occasion special and joyful.

Sick people who are unable to receive Communion under the form of bread may receive it under the form of wine alone. If the wine is consecrated at a Mass not celebrated in the presence of the sick person, the Blood of the Lord is kept in a properly covered vessel and is placed in the tabernacle after Communion. The Precious Blood should be carried to the sick in a vessel which is closed in such a way as to eliminate all danger of spilling. If some of the Precious Blood remains, it should be consumed by the minister, who should also see to it that the vessel is properly purified afterward by a Priest or Deacon.

75   If the sick wish to celebrate the Sacrament of Penance, it is preferable that the Priest make himself available for this during a previous visit.

76   If it is necessary to celebrate the Sacrament of Penance during the rite of Communion, it takes the place of the Penitential Act.

Communion in Ordinary Circumstances

77   If possible, provision should be made to celebrate Mass in the homes of the sick, with their families and friends gathered around them. The Ordinary determines the conditions and requirements for such celebrations.

Communion in a Hospital or Institution

78   There will be situations, particularly in large institutions with many communicants, when the minister should consider alternative means so that the rite of Communion of the sick is not diminished to the absolute minimum. In such cases the following alternatives should be considered: (a) where possible, the residents or patients may be gathered in groups in one or more areas; (b) additional ministers of Communion may assist.
     When it is not possible to celebrate the full rite, the rite for Communion in a hospital or institution may be used. If it is convenient, however, the minister may add elements from the rite for ordinary circumstances, for example, a Scripture reading.

79   The rite begins with the recitation of the Eucharistic antiphon in the church, the hospital chapel, or the first room visited. Then the minister gives Communion to the sick in their individual rooms.

80   The concluding prayer may be said in the church, the hospital chapel, or the last room visited. No blessing is given.

Communion in Ordinary Circumstances

Introductory Rites
Greeting

81   The minister greets the sick person and the others present. One of the following may be used:

A

Peace be with this house and with all who live here.

B

The peace of the Lord be with you.

C

The grace of our Lord Jesus Christ
and the love of God
and the communion of the Holy Spirit be with you all.

D

Grace to you and peace from God our Father
and the Lord Jesus Christ.

If the minister is not a Priest or Deacon, he or she adds to the greeting:
Blessed be God for ever, *to which all respond:*

Blessed be God for ever.

The minister then places the Blessed Sacrament on the table and all join in adoration.

PENITENTIAL ACT

83   The minister invites the sick person and all present to join in the Penitential Act, using these words:

My brothers and sisters, to prepare ourselves for this celebration, let us call to mind our sins.

After a brief period of silence, the Penitential Act continues, using one of the following:

A

All say:
I confess to almighty God,
and to you, my brothers and sisters,
that I have greatly sinned,
in my thoughts and in my words,
in what I have done, and in what I have failed to do;

And, striking their breast, they say:
through my fault, through my fault,
through my most grievous fault;

Then they continue:
therefore I ask blessed Mary ever-virgin,
all the Angels and Saints,
and you, my brothers and sisters,
to pray for me to the Lord our God.

B

Have mercy on us, O Lord.
R. *For we have sinned against you.*
Show us, O Lord, your mercy.
R. *And grant us your salvation.*

C

By your Paschal Mystery
   you have won for us salvation:
Lord, have mercy.

R. *Lord, have mercy.*

You renew among us now
   the wonders of your Passion:
Christ, have mercy.

R. *Christ, have mercy.*

When we receive your Body
you share with us your Paschal sacrifice:
Lord, have mercy.

R. *Lord, have mercy.*

The minister concludes the Penitential Act with the following:

May almighty God have mercy on us,
forgive us our sins,
and bring us to everlasting life.

R. *Amen.*

Liturgy of the Word

Reading

84   The word of God is proclaimed by one of those present or by the minister. An appropriate reading from Part III or one of the following readings may be used:

A John 6:51

B John 6:54–58

C John 14:6

D John 15:5

E 1 John 4:16

Response

85   A brief period of silence may be observed after the reading of the word of God.

The minister may then give a brief explanation of the reading, applying it to the needs of the sick person and those who are looking after him or her.

Universal Prayer

86   The Universal Prayer (Prayer of the Faithful) may be said. With a brief introduction the minister invites all those present to pray. After the intentions the minister says the concluding prayer. It is desirable that the intentions be announced by someone other than the minister.

Liturgy of Holy Communion

The Lord's Prayer

87   *The minister introduces the Lord's Prayer in these or similar words:*

A

Now let us pray as Christ the Lord has taught us:

B

And now let us pray with confidence as Christ our Lord commanded:
All say:

Our Father . . .

Communion

88   *The minister shows the Eucharistic Bread to those present, saying:*
Behold the Lamb of God,
behold him who takes away the sins of the world.
Blessed are those called to the supper of the Lamb.

The sick person and all who are to receive Communion say:
Lord, I am not worthy
that you should enter under my roof,
but only say the word
and my soul shall be healed.

The minister goes to the sick person and, showing the Blessed Sacrament, says:
The Body of Christ.

The sick person answers: Amen, *and receives Communion.*

Then if the Blood of Christ is to be given, the minister says:
The Blood of Christ.

The sick person answers: Amen, *and receives Communion. Others present who wish to receive Communion then do so in the usual way.*

Silent Prayer

89   *Then a period of silence may be observed.*

Prayer after Communion

90   *The minister says a concluding prayer. One of the following may be used:*

Let us pray.

Pause for silent prayer, if this has not preceded.

A

All-powerful and ever-living God,
may the Body and Blood of Christ your Son
be for our brother/sister **N.**
a lasting remedy for body and soul.
Through Christ our Lord.
R. *Amen.*

B

O God, who have accomplished the work of
        human redemption
through the Paschal Mystery of your Only Begotten Son,
graciously grant that we, who confidently proclaim,
under sacramental signs, the Death and Resurrection
        of Christ,
may experience continued increase of your saving grace.
Through Christ our Lord.
R. *Amen.*

C

O God, who willed that we be partakers
in the one Bread and the one Chalice,
grant us, we pray, so to live
that, made one in Christ,
we may joyfully bear fruit
for the salvation of the world.
Through Christ our Lord.

R. *Amen.*

D

Nourished by this sacred gift, O Lord,
we give you thanks and beseech your mercy,
that, by the pouring forth of your Spirit,
the grace of integrity may endure
in those your heavenly power has entered.
Through Christ our Lord.

R. *Amen.*

Concluding Rite

Blessing

91   A minister who is not a Priest or Deacon invokes God's blessing and makes the Sign of the Cross on himself or herself, while saying:

A

May the Lord bless us,
protect us from all evil,
and bring us to everlasting life.

R. *Amen.*

B

May the almighty and merciful God bless and protect us, the Father, and the Son, and the Holy Spirit.

R. *Amen.*

Communion in a Hospital or Institution

Introductory Rite

Antiphon

92   The rite may begin in the church, the hospital chapel, or the first room, where the minister says one of the following antiphons:

A

How holy this feast
in which Christ is our food:
his passion is recalled;
grace fills our hearts;
and we receive a pledge of the glory to come.

B

How gracious you are, Lord:
your gift of bread from heaven
reveals a Father's love and brings us perfect joy.
You fill the hungry with good things
and send the rich away empty.

C

I am the living bread
come down from heaven.
If you eat this bread
you will live for ever.
The bread I will give is my flesh
for the life of the world.

If it is customary, the minister may be accompanied by a person carrying a candle.

LITURGY OF HOLY COMMUNION

Greeting

93   *On entering each room, the minister may use one of the following greetings:*

A

The peace of the Lord be with you.

B

The grace of our Lord Jesus Christ
and the love of God
and the communion of the Holy Spirit be with you all.

If the minister is not a Priest or Deacon, he or she adds to the greeting:
Blessed be God for ever, *to which all respond:*

Blessed be God for ever.

The minister then places the Blessed Sacrament on the table, and all join in adoration.

If there is time and it seems desirable, the minister may proclaim a Scripture reading from those found in no. 84 or those appearing in Part III.

The Lord's Prayer

94   *When circumstances permit (for example, when there are not many rooms to visit), the minister is encouraged to lead the sick in the Lord's Prayer. The minister introduces the Lord's Prayer in these or similar words:*

A

Now let us pray as Christ the Lord has taught us:

B

And now let us pray with confidence as Christ our Lord commanded:

All say:

Our Father . . .

Communion

95 *The minister shows the Eucharistic Bread to those present, saying:*

Behold the Lamb of God,
behold him who takes away the sins of the world.
Blessed are those called to the supper of the Lamb.

The sick person and all who are to receive Communion say:

Lord, I am not worthy
that you should enter under my roof,
but only say the word
and my soul shall be healed.

The minister goes to the sick person and, showing the Blessed Sacrament, says:

The Body of Christ.

The sick person answers: Amen, *and receives Communion.*

Then if the Blood of Christ is to be given, the minister says:

The Blood of Christ.

The sick person answers: Amen, *and receives Communion.*

Others present who wish to receive Communion then do so in the usual way.

Concluding Rite

Concluding Prayer

96   The concluding prayer may be said either in the last room visited, in the church, or chapel. One of the following may be used.

Let us pray.

Pause for silent prayer, if this has not preceded.

A

All-powerful and ever-living God,
may the Body and Blood of Christ your Son
be for our brothers and sisters
a lasting remedy for body and soul.
Through Christ our Lord.

R. *Amen.*

B

O God, who have accomplished the work of human
    redemption
through the Paschal Mystery of your Only Begotten Son,
graciously grant that we, who confidently proclaim,
under sacramental signs, the Death and Resurrection
    of Christ,
may experience continued increase of your saving grace.
Through Christ our Lord.

R. *Amen.*

C

O God, who have willed that we be partakers
in the one Bread and the one Chalice,
grant us, we pray, so to live
that, made one in Christ,
we may joyfully bear fruit
for the salvation of the world.
Through Christ our Lord.

R. *Amen.*

D

Nourished by this sacred gift, O Lord,
we give you thanks and beseech your mercy,
that, by the pouring forth of your Spirit,
the grace of integrity may endure
in those your heavenly power has entered.
Through Christ our Lord.

R. *Amen.*

The blessing is omitted.

Pastoral Care of the Dying

INTRODUCTION

When we were baptized in Christ Jesus we were baptized into his death . . . so that as Christ was raised from the dead by the Father's glory, we too might live a new life.

161   The rites in Part II of *Pastoral Care of the Sick: Rites of Anointing and Viaticum* are used by the Church to comfort and strengthen a dying Christian in the passage from this life. The ministry to the dying places emphasis on trust in the Lord's promise of eternal life rather than on the struggle against illness which is characteristic of the pastoral care of the sick.

The first three chapters of Part II provide for those situations in which time is not a pressing concern and the rites can be celebrated fully and properly. These are to be clearly distinguished from the rites contained in Chapter Eight, "Rites for Exceptional Circumstances," which provide for the emergency situations sometimes encountered in the ministry to the dying.

162   Priests with pastoral responsibilities are to direct the efforts of the family and friends as well as other ministers of the local Church in the care of the dying. They should ensure that all are familiar with the rites provided here.

The words "Priest," "Deacon," and "minister" are used advisedly. Only in those rites which must be celebrated by a Priest is the word "Priest" used in the rubrics (that is, the Sacrament of Penance, the Sacrament of the Anointing of the Sick, the celebration of Viaticum within Mass). Whenever it is clear that, in the absence of a Priest, a Deacon may preside at a particular rite, the words "Priest or Deacon," are used in the rubrics. Whenever another minister is permitted to celebrate a rite in the absence of a Priest or Deacon, the word "minister" is used in the rubrics, even though in many cases the rite will be celebrated by a Priest or Deacon.

163   The Christian community has a continuing responsibility to pray for and with the person who is dying. Through its sacramental ministry to the dying the community helps Christians to embrace death in mysterious union with the crucified and risen Lord, who awaits them in the fullness of life.

Celebration of Viaticum

164   A rite for Viaticum within Mass and another for Viaticum outside Mass are provided. If possible, and with the permission of the Ordinary, Viaticum should take place within the full Eucharistic celebration, with the family, friends, and other members of the Christian community taking part. The rite for Viaticum outside Mass is used when the full Eucharistic celebration cannot take place. Again, if it is possible, others should take part.

Commendation of the Dying

165   The second chapter of Part II contains a collection of prayers for the spiritual comfort of the Christian who is close to death. These prayers are traditionally called the commendation of the dying to God and are to be used according to the circumstances of each case.

Prayers for the Dead

166   A chapter has also been provided to assist a minister who has been called to attend a person who is already dead. A Priest is not to administer the Sacrament of Anointing. Instead, he should pray for the dead person, using prayers such as those which appear in this chapter. He may find it necessary to explain to the family of the person who is dead that sacraments are celebrated for the living, not for the dead, and that the dead are effectively helped by the prayers of the living.

Rites for Exceptional Circumstances

167   Chapter Eight, "Rites for Exceptional Circumstances," contains rites which should be celebrated with a person who has suddenly been placed in proximate or immediate danger of death. They are for emergency circumstances and should be used only when such pressing conditions exist.

Care of a Dying Child

168   In its ministry to the dying the Church must also respond to the difficult circumstances of a dying child. Although no specific rites appear in Part II for the care of a dying child, these notes are provided to help bring into focus the various aspects of this ministry.

169   When parents learn that their child is dying, they are often bewildered and hurt. In their love for their son or daughter, they may be beset by temptations and doubts and find themselves asking: Why is God taking this child from us? How have we sinned or failed that God would punish us in this way? Why is this innocent child being hurt?

Under these trying circumstances, much of the Church's ministry will be directed to the parents and family. While pain and suffering in an innocent child are difficult for others to bear, the Church helps the parents and family to accept what God has allowed to happen. It should be understood by all beforehand that this process of acceptance will probably extend beyond the death of the child. The concern of the Christian community should continue as long as necessary.

Concern for the child must be equal to that for the family. Those who deal with dying children observe that their faith matures rapidly. Though young children often seem to accept death more easily than adults, they will often experience a surprisingly mature anguish because of the pain which they see in their families.

170   At such a time, it is important for members of the Christian community to come to the support of the child and the family by prayer, visits, and other forms of assistance. Those who have lost children of their own have a ministry of consolation and support to the family. Hospital personnel (doctors, nurses, aides) should also be prepared to exercise a special role with the child as caring adults. Priests and Deacons bear particular responsibility for overseeing all these elements of the Church's pastoral ministry. The minister should invite members of the community to use their individual gifts in this work of communal care and concern.

171   By conversation and brief services of readings and prayers, the minister may help the parents and family to see that their child is being called ahead of them to enter the kingdom and joy of the Lord. The period when the child is dying can become a special time of renewal and prayer for the family and close friends. The minister should help them to see that the child's sufferings are united to those of Jesus for the salvation of the whole world.

172   If it is appropriate, the Priest should discuss with the parents the possibility of preparing and celebrating with the child the Sacraments of Initiation (Baptism, Confirmation, Eucharist). The Priest may baptize and confirm the child (see *Rite of Confirmation,* no. 7b). To complete the process of Initiation, the child should also receive first Communion.

According to the circumstances, some of these rites may be celebrated by a Deacon or layperson. So that the child and family may receive full benefit from them, these rites are normally celebrated over a period of time. In this case, the minister should use the usual rites, that is, the *Rite of Baptism for Children,* the *Rite of Confirmation,* and if suitable, the *Rite of Penance.* Similarly, if time allows, the usual rites for Anointing and Viaticum should be celebrated.

173   If sudden illness or an accident has placed an uninitiated child in proximate danger of death, the minister uses "Christian Initiation for the Dying," adapting it for use with a child.

174   For an initiated child or a child lacking only the Sacrament of Confirmation, who is in proximate danger of death, the "Continuous Rite of Penance, Anointing, and Viaticum" may be used and adapted to the understanding of the child. If death is imminent it should be remembered that Viaticum rather than Anointing is the sacrament for the dying.

Celebration of Viaticum

INTRODUCTION

I am going to prepare a place for you; I shall come back and take you with me.

175 This chapter contains a rite for Viaticum within Mass and a rite for Viaticum outside Mass. The celebration of the Eucharist as Viaticum, food for the passage through death to eternal life, is the sacrament proper to the dying Christian. It is the completion and crown of the Christian life on this earth, signifying that the Christian follows the Lord to eternal glory and the banquet of the heavenly kingdom.

The Sacrament of the Anointing of the Sick should be celebrated at the beginning of a serious illness. Viaticum, celebrated when death is close, will then be better understood as the last sacrament of Christian life.

176 Priests and other ministers entrusted with the spiritual care of the sick should do everything they can to ensure that those in proximate danger of death receive the Body and Blood of Christ as Viaticum. At the earliest opportunity, the necessary preparation should be given to the dying person, family, and others who may take part.

177 Whenever it is possible, the dying Christian should be able to receive Viaticum within Mass. In this way he or she shares fully, during the final moments of this life, in the Eucharistic Sacrifice, which proclaims the Lord's own passing through death to life. However, circumstances, such as confinement to a hospital ward or the very emergency which makes death imminent, may frequently make the complete Eucharistic celebration impossible. In this case, the rite for Viaticum outside Mass is appropriate. The minister should wear attire appropriate to this ministry.

178 Because the celebration of Viaticum ordinarily takes place in the limited circumstances of the home, a hospital, or other institution,

the simplifications of the rite for Masses in small gatherings may be appropriate. Depending on the condition of the dying person, every effort should be made to involve him or her, the family, friends, and other members of the local community in the planning and celebration. Appropriate readings, prayers, and songs will help to foster the full participation of all. Because of this concern for participation, the minister should ensure that Viaticum is celebrated while the dying person is still able to take part and respond.

179   A distinctive feature of the celebration of Viaticum, whether within or outside Mass, is the renewal of the baptismal profession of faith by the dying person. This occurs after the Homily and replaces the usual form of the Profession of Faith. Through the baptismal profession at the end of earthly life, the one who is dying uses the language of his or her initial commitment, which is renewed each Easter and on other occasions in the Christian life. In the context of Viaticum, it is a renewal and fulfillment of initiation into the Christian mysteries, Baptism leading to the Eucharist.

180   The rites for Viaticum within and outside Mass may include the sign of peace. The minister and all who are present embrace the dying Christian. In this and in other parts of the celebration the sense of leave-taking need not be concealed or denied, but the joy of Christian hope, which is the comfort and strength of the one near death, should also be evident.

181   As an indication that the reception of the Eucharist by the dying Christian is a pledge of resurrection and food for the passage through death, the special words proper to Viaticum are added: "May the Lord Jesus Christ protect you and lead you to eternal life." The dying person and all who are present may receive Communion under both kinds. The sign of Communion is more complete when received in this manner because it expresses more fully and clearly the nature of the Eucharist as a meal, one which prepares all who take part in it for the heavenly banquet (see the *General Instruction of the Roman Missal,* no. 281).

   The minister should choose the manner of giving Communion under both kinds which is suitable in the particular case. If the wine is consecrated at a Mass not celebrated in the presence of the sick person, the Blood of the Lord is kept in a properly covered vessel and is placed in the tabernacle after Communion. The Precious Blood should be carried to the sick person in a vessel which is closed in such a way as to eliminate all danger of spilling. If some of the Precious Blood remains after Communion, it should be consumed by the minister, who should also see to it that the vessel is properly purified afterward by a Priest or Deacon.

The sick who are unable to receive under the form of bread may receive under the form of wine alone. If the wine is consecrated at a Mass not celebrated in the presence of the sick person, the instructions given above are followed.

182 In addition to these elements of the rites which are to be given greater stress, special texts are provided for the Universal Prayer or litany and the final Solemn Blessing.

183 It often happens that a person who has received the Eucharist as Viaticum lingers in a grave condition or at the point of death for a period of days or longer. In these circumstances he or she should be given the opportunity to receive the Eucharist as Viaticum on successive days, frequently if not daily. This may take place during or outside Mass as particular conditions permit. The rite may be simplified according to the condition of the one who is dying.

Viaticum within Mass

184 When Viaticum is received within Mass, the ritual Mass for Viaticum or the Mass of the Holy Eucharist may be celebrated. The priest wears white vestments. The readings may be taken from the *Lectionary for Mass* (second edition, nos. 796–800), unless the dying person and those involved with the Priest in planning the liturgy choose other readings from Scripture.

A ritual Mass is not permitted during the Easter Triduum, on the Solemnities of Christmas, Epiphany, Ascension, Pentecost, Corpus Christi, or on a Solemnity which is a Holyday of Obligation. On these occasions, the texts and readings are taken from the Mass of the day. Although the Mass for Viaticum or the Mass of the Holy Eucharist are also excluded on the Sundays of Advent, Lent, and Easter Time, on Solemnities, Ash Wednesday, and the weekdays of Holy Week, one of the readings may be taken from the biblical texts indicated above. The special form of the final blessing may be used and, at the discretion of the Priest, the Apostolic Pardon may be added.

185   If the dying person wishes to celebrate the Sacrament of Penance, it is preferable that the Priest make himself available for this during a previous visit. If this is not possible, the Sacrament of Penance may be celebrated before Mass begins (see Appendix, p. 372).

Viaticum outside Mass

186   Although Viaticum celebrated in the context of the full Eucharistic celebration is always preferable, when it is not possible the rite for Viaticum outside Mass is appropriate. This rite includes some of the elements of the Mass, especially a brief Liturgy of the Word. Depending on the circumstances and the condition of the dying person, this rite should also be a communal celebration. Every effort should be made to involve the dying person, family, friends, and members of the local community in the planning and celebration. The manner of celebration and the elements of the rite which are used should be accommodated to those present and the nearness of death.

187   If the dying person wishes to celebrate the Sacrament of Penance and this cannot take place during a previous visit, it should be celebrated before the rite of Viaticum begins, especially if others are present. Alternatively, it may be celebrated during the rite of Viaticum, replacing the Penitential Act. At the discretion of the Priest, the Apostolic Pardon may be added after the Penitential Act or after the Sacrament of Penance.

188   An abbreviated Liturgy of the Word, ordinarily consisting of a single biblical reading, gives the minister an opportunity to explain the word of God in relation to Viaticum. The sacrament should be described as the sacred food which strengthens the Christian for the passage through death to life in sure hope of the resurrection.

Viaticum outside Mass

Introductory Rites

Greeting

197 The minister greets the sick person and the others present. The following may be used:

A

Peace be with this house and with all who live here.

B

The peace of the Lord be with you.

C

The grace of our Lord Jesus Christ
and the love of God
and the communion of the Holy Spirit be with you all.

D

Grace to you and peace from God our Father
and the Lord Jesus Christ.

If the minister is not a Priest or Deacon, he or she adds to the greeting: Blessed be God for ever, to which all respond:

Blessed be God for ever.

The minister then places the Blessed Sacrament on the table, and all join in adoration.

Instruction

199 Afterward the minister addresses those present, using the following instruction or one better suited to the sick person's condition:

My brothers and sisters, before our Lord Jesus Christ passed from this world to return to the Father, he left us the sacrament of his Body and Blood. When the hour comes for us to pass from this life and join him, he strengthens us with this food for our journey and comforts us by this pledge of our resurrection.

Penitential Act

200 The minister invites the sick person and all present to join in the Penitential Act, using these words:

My brothers and sisters, to prepare ourselves for this celebration, let us call to mind our sins.

After a brief period of silence, the Penitential Act continues using one of the following prayers.

A *All say:*

I confess to almighty God,
and to you, my brothers and sisters,
that I have greatly sinned,
in my thoughts and in my words,
in what I have done, and in what I have failed to do;

And, striking thier breast, they say:
through my fault, through my fault,
through my most grievous fault;

Then they continue:
therefore I ask blessed Mary ever-virgin,
all the Angels and Saints,
and you, my brothers and sisters,
to pray for me to the Lord our God.

B

By your Paschal Mystery
    you have won for us salvation:
Lord, have mercy.
R. *Lord, have mercy.*

You renew among us now
    the wonders of your Passion:
Christ, have mercy.
R. *Christ, have mercy.*

When we receive your Body,
you share with us your Paschal sacrifice:
Lord, have mercy.
R. *Lord, have mercy.*

The minister concludes the Penitential Act with the following:
May almighty God have mercy us,
forgive us our sins,
and bring us to everlasting life.
R. *Amen.*

Liturgy of the Word

Reading

202 *The word of God is proclaimed by one of those present or by the minister. An appropriate reading from Part III or one of the following may be used:*

A John 6:54–55

B John 14:23

C John 15:4

D 1 Corinthians 11:26

Homily

203 *Depending on circumstances, the minister may then give a brief explanation of the reading.*

Baptismal Profession of Faith

204 *It is desirable that the sick person renew his or her baptismal profession of faith before receiving Viaticum. The minister gives a brief introduction and then asks the following questions:*

N., do you believe in God,
the Father almighty,
Creator of heaven and earth?

R. *I do.*

Do you believe in Jesus Christ, his only Son, our Lord,
who was born of the Virgin Mary,
suffered death and was buried,
rose again from the dead
and is seated at the right hand of the Father?

R. *I do.*

Do you believe in the Holy Spirit,
the holy Catholic Church,
the communion of saints,
the forgiveness of sins,
the resurrection of the body,
and life everlasting?

R. *I do.*

Litany

205   The minister may adapt or shorten the litany according to the condition of the sick person. The litany may be omitted if the sick person has made the Profession of Faith and appears to be tiring.

My brothers and sisters, with one heart let us call on our Savior Jesus Christ.

You loved us to the very end and gave yourself over to death in order to give us life. For our brother/sister, Lord, we pray:

R. *Lord, hear our prayer.*

You said to us: "All who eat my flesh and drink my blood will live for ever." For our brother/sister, Lord, we pray:

R. *Lord, hear our prayer.*

You invite us to join in the banquet where pain and sorrow, sadness and separation will be no more. For our brother/sister, Lord, we pray:

R. *Lord, hear our prayer.*

Liturgy of Viaticum

The Lord's Prayer

206   The minister introduces the Lord's Prayer in these words:

A

Now let us offer together the prayer our Lord Jesus Christ taught us:

B

And now let us pray with confidence as Christ our Lord commanded:

All say:

Our Father . . .

Communion as Viaticum

207   The sick person and all present may receive Communion under both kinds. When the minister gives Communion to the sick person, the form for Viaticum is used.

The minister shows the Eucharistic Bread to those present, saying:

Behold the Lamb of God,
behold him who takes away the sins of the world.
Blessed are those called to the supper of the Lamb.

The sick person and all who are to receive Communion say:

Lord, I am not worthy
that you should enter under my roof,
but only say the word
and my soul shall be healed.

The minister goes to the sick person and, showing the Blessed Sacrament, says:

The Body of Christ.

The sick person answers: Amen.

Then if the Blood of Christ is to be given, the minister says:

The Blood of Christ.

The sick person answers: Amen.

Immediately, or after giving Communion to the sick person, the minister adds:

May the Lord Jesus Christ protect you
and lead you to eternal life.

R. Amen.

Others present who wish to receive Communion then do so in the usual way.

After the conclusion of the rite, the minister cleanses the vessel as usual.

Silent Prayer

208   *Then a period of silence may be observed.*

Prayer after Communion

209   *The minister says the concluding prayer.*

Let us pray.

Pause for silent prayer, if this has not preceded.

A

O God, whose Son is for us the way, the truth and the life,
look lovingly upon your servant **N.**
and grant that, trusting in your promises
and strengthened by the Body of your Son,
he (she) may journey in peace to your Kingdom.
Through Christ our Lord.

R. Amen.

B

O Lord, eternal health and salvation
of those who believe in you,
grant, we pray, that your servant **N.**,
renewed by heavenly food and drink,
may safely reach your Kingdom of light and life.
Through Christ our Lord.

R. Amen.

C

All-powerful and ever-living God,
may the Body and Blood of Christ your Son
be for our brother/sister **N.**
a lasting remedy for body and soul.

Through Christ our Lord.

R. Amen.

Concluding Rites

Blessing

210   A minister who is not a Priest or Deacon invokes God's blessing and makes the Sign of the Cross on himself or herself, while saying:

A

May the Lord bless us,
protect us from all evil,
and bring us to everlasting life.

R. *Amen.*

B

May the almighty and merciful God bless and protect us,
the Father, and the Son, and the Holy Spirit.

R. *Amen.*

Sign of Peace

211   The minister and the others present may then give the sick person the sign of peace.

Commendation of the Dying

INTRODUCTION

Into your hands, Lord, I commend my spirit.

212   In Viaticum the dying person is united with Christ in his passage out of this world to the Father. Through the prayers for the commendation of the dying contained in this chapter, the Church helps to sustain this union until it is brought to fulfillment after death.

213   Christians have the responsibility of expressing their union in Christ by joining the dying person in prayer for God's mercy and for confidence in Christ. In particular, the presence of a Priest or Deacon shows more clearly that the Christian dies in the communion of the Church. He should assist the dying person and those present in the recitation of the prayers of commendation and, following death, he should lead those present in the prayer after death. If the Priest or Deacon is unable to be present because of other serious pastoral obligations, other members of the community should be prepared to assist with these prayers and should have the texts readily available to them.

214   The minister may choose texts from among the prayers, litanies, aspirations, psalms, and readings provided in this chapter, or others may be added. In the selection of these texts the minister should keep in mind the condition and piety of both the dying person and the members of the family who are present. The prayers are best said in a slow, quiet voice, alternating with periods of silence. If possible, the minister says one or more of the brief prayer formulas with the dying person. These may be softly repeated two or three times.

215   These texts are intended to help the dying person, if still conscious, to face the natural human anxiety about death by imitating

Christ in his patient suffering and dying. The Christian will be helped to surmount his or her fear in the hope of heavenly life and resurrection through the power of Christ, who destroyed the power of death by his own dying.

Even if the dying person is not conscious, those who are present will draw consolation from these prayers and come to a better understanding of the paschal character of Christian death. This may be visibly expressed by making the Sign of the Cross on the forehead of the dying person, who was first signed with the cross at Baptism.

216   Immediately after death has occurred, all may kneel while one of those present leads the prayers given on nos. 221–222.

SHORT TEXTS

217   One or more of the following short texts may be recited with the dying person. If necessary, they may be softly repeated two or three times.

Romans 8:35
Who can separate us from the love of Christ?

Romans 14:8
Whether we live or die, we are the Lord's.

2 Corinthians 5:1
We have an everlasting home in heaven.

1 Thessalonians 4:17
We shall be with the Lord for ever.

1 John 3:2
We shall see God as he really is.

1 John 3:14
We have passed from death to life
because we love each other.

Psalm 25:1
To you, Lord, I lift up my soul.

Psalm 27:1
The Lord is my light and my salvation.

Psalm 27:13
I believe that I shall see the goodness of the Lord
in the land of the living.

Psalm 42:3
My soul thirsts for the living God.

Psalm 23:4
Though I walk in the shadow of death,
I will fear no evil, for you are with me.

Matthew 25:34
Come, blessed of my Father,
says the Lord Jesus,
and take possession of the kingdom
prepared for you.

Luke 23:43
The Lord Jesus says,
today you will be with me in paradise.

John 14:2
In my Father's home
there are many dwelling places,
says the Lord Jesus.

John 14:2–3
The Lord Jesus says,
I go to prepare a place for you,
and I will come again to take you to myself.

John 17:24
I desire that where I am,
they also may be with me,
says the Lord Jesus.

John 6:40
Everyone who believes in the Son
has eternal life.

Psalm 31:6a
Into your hands, Lord,
I commend my spirit.

Acts 7:59
Lord Jesus, receive my spirit.

Holy Mary, pray for me.

Saint Joseph, pray for me.

Jesus, Mary, and Joseph,
assist me in my last agony.

Reading

218   The word of God is proclaimed by one of those present or by the minister. Selections from Part III or from the following readings may be used:

A. *Job 19:23–27*
Job's act of faith is a model for our own; God is the God of the living.

B. *Psalm 23*

C. *Psalm 25*

D. *Psalm 91*

E. *Psalm 121*

F. *1 John 4:16*

G. *Revelation 21:1–5a, 6–7*
God our Father is the God of newness of life; it is his desire that we should come to share his life with him.

H. *Matthew 25:1–13*
Jesus bid us be prepared for our ultimate destiny, which is eternal life.

I. *Luke 22:39–46*
Jesus is alive to our pain and sorrow, because faithfulness to his Father's will cost him life itself.

J. *Luke 23:44–49*
Jesus' death is witnessed by his friends.

K. *Luke 24:1-8*
Jesus is alive; he gives us eternal life with the Father.

L. *John 6:37-40*
Jesus will raise his own from death and give them eternal life.

M. *John 14:1-6, 23, 27*
The love of Jesus can raise us up from the sorrow of death to the joy of eternal life.

Litany of the Saints

219   When the condition of the dying person calls for the use of brief forms of prayer, those who are present are encouraged to pray the Litany of the Saints—or at least some of its invocations—for him or her. Special mention may be made of the Patron Saints of the dying person, of the family, and of the parish. The Litany may be said or sung in the usual way. Other customary prayers may also be used.

A

Lord, have mercy	*Lord, have mercy*
Christ, have mercy	*Christ, have mercy*
Lord, have mercy	*Lord, have mercy*
Holy Mary, Mother of God	*pray for him/her*
Holy Angels of God	*pray for him/her*
Abraham, our father in faith	*pray for him/her*
David, leader of God's people	*pray for him/her*
All holy patriarchs and prophets	*pray for him/her*
Saint John the Baptist	*pray for him/her*
Saint Joseph	*pray for him/her*
Saint Peter and Saint Paul	*pray for him/her*
Saint Andrew	*pray for him/her*
Saint John	*pray for him/her*
Saint Mary Magdalene	*pray for him/her*

Saint Stephen.	*pray for him/her*
Saint Ignatius	*pray for him/her*
Saint Lawrence	*pray for him/her*
Saint Perpetua and Saint Felicity	*pray for him/her*
Saint Agnes	*pray for him/her*
Saint Gregory	*pray for him/her*
Saint Augustine	*pray for him/her*
Saint Athanasius.	*pray for him/her*
Saint Basil	*pray for him/her*
Saint Martin	*pray for him/her*
Saint Benedict.	*pray for him/her*
Saint Francis and Saint Dominic	*pray for him/her*
Saint Francis Xavier.	*pray for him/her*
Saint John Vianney	*pray for him/her*
Saint Catherine.	*pray for him/her*
Saint Teresa	*pray for him/her*

Other Saints may be included here.

All holy men and women.	*pray for him/her*
Lord, be merciful	*Lord, save your people*
From all evil	*Lord, save your people*
From every sin	*Lord, save your people*
From Satan's power	*Lord, save your people*
At the moment of death.	*Lord, save your people*
From everlasting death	*Lord, save your people*
On the day of judgment.	*Lord, save your people*
By your coming as man.	*Lord, save your people*
By your suffering and Cross	*Lord, save your people*
By your Death and rising to new life	*Lord, save your people*

By your return in glory
> to the Father .... *Lord, save your people*

By your gift
> of the Holy Spirit .... *Lord, save your people*

By your coming again
> in glory. .... *Lord, save your people*

Be merciful to us sinners .... *Lord, hear our prayer*

Bring *N.* to eternal life,
> first promised to
> him/her in Baptism .... *Lord, hear our prayer*

Raise *N.* on the last day,
> for he/she has eaten
> the Bread of life. .... *Lord, hear our prayer*

Let *N.* share in your glory,
> for he/she has shared
> in your suffering
> and Death .... *Lord, hear our prayer*

Jesus, Son of the living God. .... *Lord, hear our prayer*

Christ, hear us. .... *Christ, hear us*

Lord Jesus, hear our prayer .... *Lord, hear our prayer*

B

A brief form of the Litany may be prayed. Other Saints may be added, including the Patron Saints of the dying person, of the family, and of the parish; Saints to whom the dying person may have a special devotion may also be included.

Holy Mary, Mother of God .... *pray for him/her*
Holy Angels of God .... *pray for him/her*
Saint John the Baptist. .... *pray for him/her*
Saint Joseph. .... *pray for him/her*
Saint Peter and Saint Paul .... *pray for him/her*

Other Saints may be included here.

All holy men and women. . . . . *pray for him/her*

Prayer of Commendation

220 When the moment of death seems near, some of the following prayers may be said:

A

Go forth, Christian soul, from this world
in the name of God the almighty Father,
who created you,
in the name of Jesus Christ, Son of the living God,
who suffered for you,
in the name of the Holy Spirit,
who was poured out upon you,
go forth, faithful Christian.

May you live in peace this day,
may your home be with God in Zion,
with Mary, the virgin Mother of God,
with Joseph, and all the Angels and Saints.

B

I commend you, my dear brother/sister,
to almighty God,
and entrust you to your Creator.
May you return to him
who formed you from the dust of the earth.
May holy Mary, the Angels, and all the Saints
come to meet you as you go forth from this life.

May Christ who was crucified for you
bring you freedom and peace.
May Christ who died for you
admit you into his garden of paradise.
May Christ, the true Shepherd,
acknowledge you as one of his flock.
May he forgive all your sins,
and set you among those he has chosen.
May you see your Redeemer face to face,
and enjoy the vision of God for ever.
R. *Amen.*

C

Welcome your servant, Lord, into the place of salvation which because of your mercy he/she rightly hoped for.

R. *Amen,* or **R.** *Lord, save your people.*

Deliver your servant, Lord, from every distress.

R. *Amen,* or **R.** *Lord, save your people.*

Deliver your servant, Lord, as you delivered Noah
from the flood.

R. *Amen,* or **R.** *Lord, save your people.*

Deliver your servant, Lord, as you delivered Abraham from
Ur of the Chaldees.

R. *Amen,* or **R.** *Lord, save your people.*

Deliver your servant, Lord, as you delivered Moses
from the hand of the Pharaoh.

R. *Amen,* or **R.** *Lord, save your people.*

Deliver your servant, Lord, as you delivered Daniel
from the den of lions.

R. *Amen,* or **R.** *Lord, save your people.*

Deliver your servant, Lord, as you delivered the three young
men from the fiery furnace.

R. *Amen,* or **R.** *Lord, save your people.*

Deliver your servant, Lord, as you delivered Susanna
from her false accusers.

R. *Amen,* or **R.** *Lord, save your people.*

Deliver your servant, Lord, as you delivered David
from the attacks of Saul and Goliath.

R. *Amen,* or **R.** *Lord, save your people.*

Deliver your servant, Lord, as you delivered Peter and Paul
from prison.

R. *Amen,* or **R.** *Lord, save your people.*

Deliver your servant, Lord, through Jesus our Savior,
who suffered death for us and gave us eternal life.

R. *Amen,* or **R.** *Lord, save your people.*

D

Lord Jesus Christ, Savior of the world,
we pray for your servant **N.**,
and commend him/her to your mercy.
For his/her sake you came down from heaven;
receive him/her now into the joy of your kingdom.

For though he/she has sinned,
he/she has not denied the Father, the Son, and the Holy Spirit,
but has believed in God
and has worshipped his/her Creator.

R. *Amen.*

E   *The following antiphon may be said or sung:*

Hail, holy Queen, Mother of mercy,
hail, our life, our sweetness, and our hope.
To you we cry, the children of Eve;
to you we send up our sighs,
mourning and weeping in this land of exile.
Turn, then, most gracious advocate,
your eyes of mercy toward us;
lead us home at last
and show us the blessed fruit of your womb, Jesus:
O clement, O loving, O sweet Virgin Mary.

Prayer after Death

221 When death has occurred, one or more of the following prayers may be said:

A

Saints of God, come to his/her aid!
Come to meet him/her, Angels of the Lord!

R. *Receive his/her soul and present him/her to God the Most High.*

May Christ, who called you, take you to himself;
may Angels lead you to Abraham's side.

R. *Receive his/her soul and present him/her to God the Most High.*

Give him/her eternal rest, O Lord,
and may your light shine on him/her for ever.

R. *Receive his/her soul and present him/her to God the Most High.*

The following prayer is added:

Let us pray.

All-powerful and merciful God,
we commend to you **N.**, your servant.
In your mercy and love,
blot out the sins he/she has committed
   through human weakness.
In this world he/she has died:
let him/her live with you for ever.
Through Christ our Lord.

R. *Amen.*

For the solace of those present the minister may conclude these prayers with a simple blessing or with a symbolic gesture, for example, signing the forehead with the Sign of the Cross.

B PSALM 130

R. *My soul hopes in the Lord.*

Out of the depths I cry to you, O Lord;
  Lord, hear my voice!
Let your ears be attentive
  to my voice in supplication. **R.**

I trust in the Lord,
  my soul trusts in his word.
My soul waits for the Lord
  more than sentinels wait for the dawn. **R.**

For with the Lord is kindness,
  and with him is plenteous redemption.
And he will redeem Israel
  from all their iniquities. **R.**

The following prayer is added:

Let us pray.
God of love,
welcome into your presence
your son/daughter **N.**, whom you have
    called from this life.
Release him/her from all his/her sins,
bless him/her with eternal light and peace,
raise him/her up to live for ever with all your Saints
in the glory of the resurrection.

Through Christ our Lord.
R. Amen.

C   PSALM 23

R. *Lord, remember me in your kingdom.*

The LORD is my shepherd; I shall not want.
    In verdant pastures he gives me repose;
Beside restful waters he leads me;
    he refreshes my soul. **R.**

He guides me in right paths
    for his name's sake.
Even though I walk in the dark valley
    I fear no evil; for you are at my side
With your rod and your staff
    that give me courage. **R.**

You spread the table before me
   in the sight of my foes;
You anoint my head with oil;
   my cup overflows. **R.**

Only goodness and kindness follow me
   all the days of my life;
And I shall dwell in the house of the Lord
   for years to come. **R.**

The following prayer is added:
Let us pray.
God of mercy,
hear our prayers and be merciful
to your son/daughter **N.**,
   whom you have called from this life.
Welcome him/her into the company of your Saints,
in the kingdom of light and peace.

Through Christ our Lord.
R. *Amen.*

D
Almighty and eternal God,
hear our prayers for your son/daughter **N.**,
whom you have called from this life to yourself.
Grant him/her light, happiness, and peace.
Let him/her pass in safety through the gates
of death,
and live for ever with all your Saints
in the light you promised to Abraham
and to all his descendants in faith.

Guard him/her from all harm
and on that great day of resurrection and reward
raise him/her up with all your Saints.
Pardon his/her sins
and give him/her eternal life in your kingdom.

Through Christ our Lord.
R. *Amen.*

E
Loving and merciful God,
we entrust our brother/sister to your mercy.
You loved him/her greatly in this life:
now that he/she is freed from all its cares,
give him/her happiness and peace for ever.

The old order has passed away:
welcome him/her now into paradise
where there will be no more sorrow,
no more weeping or pain,
but only peace and joy

with Jesus, your Son,
and the Holy Spirit
for ever and ever.
R. *Amen.*

F

God of our destiny,
into your hands we commend our brother/sister.
We are confident that with all who have died in Christ
he/she will be raised to life on the last day
and live with Christ for ever.

[We thank you for all the blessings
you gave him/her in this life
to show your fatherly care for all of us
and the fellowship which is ours with the Saints in Jesus Christ.]

Lord, hear our prayer:
welcome our brother/sister to paradise
and help us to comfort each other
with the assurance of our faith
until we all meet in Christ
to be with you and with our brother/sister for ever.

Through Christ our Lord.
R. *Amen.*

Prayer for the Family and Friends

222   *The following prayer may be said:*

Let us pray.

A   *For the family and friends*

God of all consolation,
in your unending love and mercy for us
you turn the darkness of death
into the dawn of new life.
Show compassion to your people in their sorrow.
[Be our refuge and our strength
to lift us from the darkness of this grief
to the peace and light of your presence.]
Your Son, our Lord Jesus Christ,
by dying for us, conquered death
and by rising again, restored life.
May we then go forward eagerly to meet him,
and after our life on earth
be reunited with our brothers and sisters
where every tear will be wiped away.
Through Christ our Lord.

R. *Amen.*

B *For the deceased person and for family and friends*

Lord Jesus, our Redeemer,
you willingly gave yourself up to death
so that all people might be saved
and pass from death into new life.
Listen to our prayers,
look with love on your people
who mourn and pray for their brother/sister *N*.

Lord Jesus, holy and compassionate:
forgive *N*. his/her sins.
By dying you opened the gates of life
for those who believe in you:
do not let our brother/sister be parted from you,
but by your glorious power
give him/her light, joy, and peace in heaven
where you live for ever and ever.
R. *Amen.*

For the solace of those present the minister may conclude these prayers with a simple blessing or with a symbolic gesture, for example, signing the forehead with the Sign of the Cross.

Prayers for the Dead

INTRODUCTION

I want those you have given me to be with me where I am.

223   This chapter contains prayers for use by a minister who has been called to attend a person who is already dead. A Priest is not to administer the Sacraments of Penance or Anointing. Instead, he should pray for the dead person using these or similar prayers.

224   It may be necessary to explain to the family of the person who is dead that sacraments are celebrated for the living, not for the dead, and that the dead are effectively helped by the prayers of the living.

225   To comfort those present the minister may conclude these prayers with a simple blessing or with a symbolic gesture, for example, making the Sign of the Cross on the forehead. A Priest or Deacon may sprinkle the body with holy water.

Greeting
226   The minister greets those who are present, offering them sympathy and the consolation of faith, using the following or similar words:

A

In this moment of sorrow
the Lord is in our midst
and comforts us with his word:
Blessed are the sorrowful; they shall be consoled.

B

Praised be God, the Father of our Lord Jesus Christ,
the Father of mercies,
and the God of all consolation!
He comforts us in all our afflictions
and thus enables us to comfort those who are in trouble,
with the same consolation
we have received from him.

Prayer

227   The minister then says one of the following prayers, commending the person who has just died to God's mercy and goodness:

Let us pray.

A

Almighty and eternal God,
hear our prayers for your son/daughter **N.**,
whom you have called from this life to yourself.

Grant him/her light, happiness, and peace.
Let him/her pass in safety through the gates of death,
and live for ever with all your Saints
in the light you promised to Abraham
and to all his descendants in faith.

Guard him/her from all harm
and on that great day of resurrection and reward
raise him/her up with all your Saints.
Pardon his/her sins
and give him/her eternal life in your kingdom.

Through Christ our Lord.

R. *Amen.*

B

Loving and merciful God,
we entrust our brother/sister to your mercy.
You loved him/her greatly in this life:
now that he/she is freed from all its cares,
give him/her happiness and peace for ever.

The old order has passed away:
welcome him/her now into paradise
where there will be no more sorrow,
no more weeping or pain,
but only peace and joy
with Jesus, your Son,
and the Holy Spirit
for ever and ever.

R. Amen.

Reading

228   The word of God is proclaimed by one of those present or by the minister. One of the following readings may be used:

A Luke 23:44–46
B John 11:3–7, 20–27, 33–36, 41–44

Litany

229 Then one of those present may lead the others in praying a brief form of the Litany of the Saints. (The full form of the Litany of the Saints may be found in no. 219.) Other Saints may be added, including the Patron Saints of the dead person, of the family, and of the parish; Saints to whom the deceased person may have had a special devotion may also be included.

Saints of God, come to his/her aid!
Come to meet him/her, Angels of the Lord!

Holy Mary, Mother of God . . . . *pray for him/her*
Saint Joseph . . . . *pray for him/her*
Saint Peter and Saint Paul . . . . *pray for him/her*

The following prayer is added:

God of mercy,
hear our prayers and be merciful
to your son/daughter **N.**, whom you have called from this life.
Welcome him/her into the company of your Saints,
in the kingdom of light and peace.

Through Christ our Lord.

R. *Amen.*

The Lord's Prayer

230 The minister introduces the Lord's Prayer in these or similar words:

A

With God there is mercy and fullness of redemption; let us pray as Jesus taught us to pray:

Prayers for the Dead

B

Let us pray for the coming of the kingdom as Jesus taught us:
All say:

Our Father . . .

Prayer of Commendation

231   *The minister then concludes with the following prayer:*

Lord Jesus, our Redeemer,
you willingly gave yourself up to death
so that all people might be saved
and pass from death into a new life.
Listen to our prayers,
look with love on your people
who mourn and pray for their brother/sister **N.**

Lord Jesus, holy and compassionate:
forgive **N.** his/her sins.
By dying you opened the gates of life
for those who believe in you:
do not let our brother/sister be parted from you,
but by your glorious power
give him/her light, joy, and peace in heaven
where you live for ever and ever.

R. Amen.

For the solace of those present the minister may conclude these prayers with a simple blessing or with a symbolic gesture, for example, signing the forehead with the Sign of the Cross.

THE GOSPEL AND EXPLANATIONS OF THE READING

ADVENT

December 3, 2023

First Sunday of Advent

A reading from the holy Gospel according to Mark   13:33–37

Jesus said to his disciples:
"Be watchful! Be alert!
You do not know when the time will come.
It is like a man traveling abroad.
He leaves home and places his servants in charge,
   each with his own work,
   and orders the gatekeeper to be on the watch.
Watch, therefore;
   you do not know when the lord of the house is coming,
   whether in the evening, or at midnight,
   or at cockcrow, or in the morning.
May he not come suddenly and find you sleeping.
What I say to you, I say to all: 'Watch!'"

The Gospel of the Lord.

Explanation of the Reading

Is living in fear the same as being watchful? Fearful people often exhibit prejudice against other races or social classes. Fearful Christians focus on their sins and hell. Jesus instructs his followers to "Be watchful," "Be alert," and "You do not know when the time will come." He is not counseling fear. Something wonderful is coming and already is. It is variously called God's kingdom, God's sovereignty, and God's reign. In the household of God, the Master is mercy and kindness. The servants stay awake because they are eager to see his return, and they want to please him by having done well.

December 8, 2023

Solemnity of the Immaculate Conception of the Blessed Virgin Mary

A reading from the holy Gospel according to Luke 1:26–38

The angel Gabriel was sent from God
 to a town of Galilee called Nazareth,
 to a virgin betrothed to a man named Joseph,
 of the house of David,
 and the virgin's name was Mary.
And coming to her, he said,
 "Hail, full of grace! The Lord is with you."
But she was greatly troubled at what was said
 and pondered what sort of greeting this might be.
Then the angel said to her,
 "Do not be afraid, Mary,
 for you have found favor with God.
Behold, you will conceive in your womb and bear a son,
 and you shall name him Jesus.
He will be great and will be called Son of
  the Most High,
 and the Lord God will give him the throne of
  David his father,
 and he will rule over the house of Jacob forever,
 and of his Kingdom there will be no end."
But Mary said to the angel,
 "How can this be,
 since I have no relations with a man?"
And the angel said to her in reply,
 "The Holy Spirit will come upon you,
 and the power of the Most High will overshadow you.

Therefore the child to be born
>   will be called holy, the Son of God.
And behold, Elizabeth, your relative,
>   has also conceived a son in her old age,
>   and this is the sixth month for her who was called barren;
>   for nothing will be impossible for God."
Mary said, "Behold, I am the handmaid of the Lord.
May it be done to me according to your word."
Then the angel departed from her.

The Gospel of the Lord.

Explanation of the Reading

The Immaculate Conception is a privilege granted to Mary in anticipation of her singular role as mother of Jesus Christ. By God's grace, the taint or shame ascribed to all humanity by the rebellion of the first human beings, Adam and Eve, was not accorded to her from her conception. Human beings view the world in linear or historical time. God, of course, sees all at once. God chose Mary in Christ before the world began to be holy and blameless in his sight, to be full of love. All human beings are redeemed by Christ, including Mary. The fullness of God's grace, though, was given to Mary at her conception. For the rest of us, grace comes after baptism.

December 10, 2023

SECOND SUNDAY OF ADVENT

A reading from the holy Gospel according to Mark 1:1–8

The beginning of the gospel of Jesus Christ
    the Son of God.

As it is written in Isaiah the prophet:
    Behold, I am sending my messenger ahead of you;
    he will prepare your way.
    A voice of one crying out in the desert:
    "Prepare the way of the Lord,
    make straight his paths."
John the Baptist appeared in the desert
    proclaiming a baptism of repentance for
        the forgiveness of sins.
People of the whole Judean countryside
    and all the inhabitants of Jerusalem
    were going out to him
        and were being baptized by him in the Jordan River
    as they acknowledged their sins.
John was clothed in camel's hair,
    with a leather belt around his waist.
He fed on locusts and wild honey.
And this is what he proclaimed:
    "One mightier than I is coming after me.
I am not worthy to stoop and loosen the thongs
    of his sandals.
I have baptized you with water;
    he will baptize you with the Holy Spirit."

The Gospel of the Lord.

Explanation of the Reading

The Gospel according to Mark has no infancy narrative. Like an archer, Mark directs his arrow to the heart of the matter. John the Baptist was the herald of the Messiah. How can believers trust this? He did what Isaiah prophesied. He wore a hairy animal skin and leather girdle. He did not point to himself but to the Coming One. He lived as an ascetic to prepare himself, and he invited the people to prepare themselves through repentance. This is the essence of the spirituality of Advent. We listen to John to stir our hope. We celebrate the sacrament of reconciliation. We pray, fast, and give—not as exercises of conversion as during Lent but to embody and bear witness to our hope.

December 17, 2023

Third Sunday of Advent

A reading from the holy Gospel according to John 1:6–8, 19–28

A man named John was sent from God.
He came for testimony, to testify to the light,
   so that all might believe through him.
He was not the light,
   but came to testify to the light.

And this is the testimony of John.
When the Jews from Jerusalem sent priests and
     Levites to him
   to ask him, "Who are you?"
   he admitted and did not deny it,
   but admitted, "I am not the Christ."
So they asked him,
   "What are you then? Are you Elijah?"
And he said, "I am not."
"Are you the Prophet?"

He answered, "No."
So they said to him,
> "Who are you, so we can give an answer to those who sent us?
What do you have to say for yourself?"
He said:
> "I am *the voice of one crying out in the desert,*
> *'make straight the way of the Lord,'*
> as Isaiah the prophet said."
Some Pharisees were also sent.
They asked him,
> "Why then do you baptize
> if you are not the Christ or Elijah or the Prophet?"
John answered them,
> "I baptize with water;
> but there is one among you
> > whom you do not recognize,
> the one who is coming after me,
> whose sandal strap I am not worthy to untie."
This happened in Bethany across the Jordan,
> where John was baptizing.

The Gospel of the Lord.

Explanation of the Reading

If someone asks, "Who are you?" it is unlikely you will answer, "I am not Santa Claus," "I am not the president. We identify ourselves by what we are, and not by what we are not. John the Baptist was careful to draw attention away from himself. "He must increase, I must decrease" (John 3:30). As human beings, we want to be known by who we are and what we do. As Christians, we must not let that need crowd out Christ. Like John, let us testify to the true Light and not to ourselves.

December 24, 2023

Fourth Sunday of Advent

A reading from the holy Gospel according to Luke 1:26–38

The angel Gabriel was sent from God
    to a town of Galilee called Nazareth,
    to a virgin betrothed to a man named Joseph,
    of the house of David,
    and the virgin's name was Mary.
And coming to her, he said,
    "Hail, full of grace! The Lord is with you."
But she was greatly troubled at what was said
    and pondered what sort of greeting this might be.
Then the angel said to her,
    "Do not be afraid, Mary,
    for you have found favor with God.

"Behold, you will conceive in your womb
    and bear a son,
    and you shall name him Jesus.
He will be great and will be called Son
    of the Most High,
    and the Lord God will give him the throne of David
        his father,
    and he will rule over the house of Jacob forever,
    and of his kingdom there will be no end."
But Mary said to the angel,
    "How can this be,
    since I have no relations with a man?"

And the angel said to her in reply,
> "The Holy Spirit will come upon you,
> and the power of the Most High
>> will overshadow you.
> Therefore the child to be born
>> will be called holy, the Son of God.
> And behold, Elizabeth, your relative,
>> has also conceived a son in her old age,
> and this is the sixth month for her
>> who was called barren;
> for nothing will be impossible for God."

Mary said, "Behold, I am the handmaid of the Lord.
May it be done to me according to your word."
Then the angel departed from her.

The Gospel of the Lord.

Explanation of the Reading

The Annunciation to Mary is one of the most frequent subjects of the great the masters of the Renaissance. However, the paintings usually reflect the culture of the master's own time. Mary is often lavishly dressed, kneeling at a prie-dieu, reading from a prayer book. The ceiling is high, perhaps with clerestory windows. None of this accurately reflects the simplicity of the original event: a very young, perhaps teenaged girl, visited by a divine messenger, invited to answer yes to God. The celebration of Christmas can overwhelm us with its sumptuousness. Focusing on Mary's experience and response is needed for us to regain perspective.

Christmas Time

December 24 and 25, 2023

Solemnity of the Nativity of the Lord (Christmas)

A reading from the holy Gospel according to Luke 2:1–14

In those days a decree went out from Caesar Augustus
   that the whole world should be enrolled.
This was the first enrollment,
   when Quirinius was governor of Syria.
So all went to be enrolled, each to his own town.
And Joseph too went up from Galilee from the town
     of Nazareth
   to Judea, to the city of David
     that is called Bethlehem,
   because he was of the house and family of David,
   to be enrolled with Mary, his betrothed,
     who was with child.
While they were there,
   the time came for her to have her child,
   and she gave birth to her firstborn son.
She wrapped him in swaddling clothes and laid him in
     a manger,
   because there was no room for them in the inn.

Now there were shepherds in that region living
> in the fields
> and keeping the night watch over their flock.
The angel of the Lord appeared to them
> and the glory of the Lord shone around them,
> and they were struck with great fear.
The angel said to them,
> "Do not be afraid;
> for behold, I proclaim to you good news of great joy
> that will be for all the people.
For today in the city of David
> a savior has been born for you who is Christ and Lord.
And this will be a sign for you:
> you will find an infant wrapped in swaddling clothes
> and lying in a manger."
And suddenly there was a multitude of the heavenly host with
> the angel,
> praising God and saying:
> > "Glory to God in the highest
> > > and on earth peace to those on whom his
> > > > favor rests."

The Gospel of the Lord.

This reading is from the Mass during the Night.

EXPLANATION OF THE READING

Today we join the shepherds who went "in haste" to see the Christ child. We join the shepherds in giving glory to God for the wonders he has performed in revealing the fullness of divine life in the innocence of human birth. We join the shepherds in praising God for his utter vulnerability, appearing in a humble manger rather than a royal throne. "Glory to God in the highest, and on earth peace to people of good will!"

December 31, 2023

FEAST OF THE HOLY FAMILY OF JESUS, MARY, AND JOSEPH

A reading from the holy Gospel according to Luke   2:22, 39–40

When the days were completed for their purification
  according to the law of Moses,
  they took him up to Jerusalem
  to present him to the Lord.

When they had fulfilled all the prescriptions
  of the law of the Lord,
  they returned to Galilee,
  to their own town of Nazareth.
The child grew and became strong, filled with wisdom;
  and the favor of God was upon him.

The Gospel of the Lord.

Longer form: Luke 2:22 – 40

EXPLANATION OF THE READING

Other than Luke's account of twelve-year-old Jesus found in the Temple, the only knowledge we have of Jesus' youth and pre-ministry adulthood is summarized in this short passage. Other than mere conjecture, nothing reliably documents those years. We know that Jesus learned Joseph's craft. As a Jewish boy, he studied the Scriptures in the home and perhaps a synagogue class. In Jewish families, there was no separation of religious and secular existence. The God of Israel was a presence in the home and daily life. Unfortunately, faith and daily life do not share common ground in today's world. Families and communities are all the poorer for it.

January 7, 2024

The Solemnity of the Epiphany of the Lord

A reading from the holy Gospel according to Matthew   2:1–12

When Jesus was born in Bethlehem of Judea,
   in the days of King Herod,
   behold, magi from the east arrived in Jerusalem, saying,
   "Where is the newborn king of the Jews?
We saw his star at its rising
   and have come to do him homage."
When King Herod heard this,
   he was greatly troubled,
   and all Jerusalem with him.
Assembling all the chief priests and the scribes
     of the people,
   he inquired of them where the Christ was to be born.
They said to him, "In Bethlehem of Judea,
   for thus it has been written through the prophet:
   And you, Bethlehem, land of Judah,
     are by no means least among the rulers of Judah;
   since from you shall come a ruler,
   who is to shepherd my people Israel."
Then Herod called the magi secretly
   and ascertained from them the time
     of the star's appearance.
He sent them to Bethlehem and said,
   "Go and search diligently for the child.
When you have found him, bring me word,
   that I too may go and do him homage."
After their audience with the king they set out.

And behold, the star that they had seen at its rising
> preceded them,
until it came and stopped over the place
> where the child was.
They were overjoyed at seeing the star,
> and on entering the house
> they saw the child with Mary his mother.
They prostrated themselves and did him homage.
Then they opened their treasures
> and offered him gifts of gold, frankincense, and myrrh.
And having been warned in a dream not to return to Herod,
> they departed for their country by another way.

The Gospel of the Lord.

Explanation of the Reading

The story of the Magi traditionally raises questions about the gifts these foreigners bring—gold, frankincense, and myrrh. They are symbolically interpreted as reflecting the Child's character and destiny: gold for royalty, frankincense for divinity, and myrrh for his humanity and anointing after death. Besides celebrating the welcoming of Gentiles into God's eternal plan, we might consider what we often forget about the foreigner, the stranger, and the culturally and religiously "other." They bring gifts and enrichment to our community, culture, and religion. Those who seek to fence out "the other" are often depriving themselves of unimagined blessings.

ORDINARY TIME DURING WINTER

January 14, 2024

SECOND SUNDAY IN ORDINARY TIME

A reading from the holy Gospel according to John 1:35–42

John was standing with two of his disciples,
   and as he watched Jesus walk by, he said,
   "Behold, the Lamb of God."
The two disciples heard what he said
   and followed Jesus.
Jesus turned and saw them following him
   and said to them,
  "What are you looking for?"
They said to him, "Rabbi"—which translated
   means Teacher—,
  "where are you staying?"
He said to them, "Come, and you will see."
So they went and saw where Jesus was staying,
   and they stayed with him that day.
It was about four in the afternoon.
Andrew, the brother of Simon Peter,
   was one of the two who heard John
     and followed Jesus.

He first found his own brother Simon and told him,
  "We have found the Messiah"—which is
    translated Christ.
Then he brought him to Jesus.
Jesus looked at him and said,
  "You are Simon the son of John;
  you will be called Cephas"—which is
    translated Peter.

The Gospel of the Lord.

EXPLANATION OF THE READING

John's account of the call of the first disciples is a story of people being led to Jesus. Andrew encounters the Lord and runs off to bring Peter back to him. John's Gospel is a reminder that the making of the disciples is the work of a community. We have the responsibility of making Jesus known to others, of bringing people to him, and of supporting each other's baptismal call.

January 21, 2024

THIRD SUNDAY IN ORDINARY TIME

A reading from the holy Gospel according to Mark   1:14–20

After John had been arrested,
    Jesus came to Galilee proclaiming the gospel of God:
    "This is the time of fulfillment.
The kingdom of God is at hand.
Repent, and believe in the gospel."

As he passed by the Sea of Galilee,
    he saw Simon and his brother Andrew casting their nets
       into the sea;
    they were fishermen.
Jesus said to them,
    "Come after me, and I will make you fishers of men."
Then they abandoned their nets and followed him.
He walked along a little farther
    and saw James, the son of Zebedee,
       and his brother John.
They too were in a boat mending their nets.
Then he called them.
So they left their father Zebedee in the boat
    along with the hired men and followed him.

The Gospel of the Lord.

EXPLANATION OF THE READING

Mark wants to convey a sense of urgency about discipleship. The first four apostles were fishers. Simon and Andrew immediately abandoned their nets. The sons of Zebedee abandoned their father in the boat. Some things in life require thoughtful reflection and time. Obedience to God's call should be at once. St. Benedict regards instant response as the first step of humility. When God's will is manifested, we must not hesitate.

January 28, 2024

Fourth Sunday in Ordinary Time

A reading from the holy Gospel according to Mark 1:21–28

Then they came to Capernaum,
   and on the sabbath Jesus entered the synagogue
     and taught.
The people were astonished at his teaching,
   for he taught them as one having authority
     and not as the scribes.
In their synagogue was a man with an unclean spirit;
   he cried out, "What have you to do with us,
     Jesus of Nazareth?
Have you come to destroy us?
I know who you are — the Holy One of God!"
Jesus rebuked him and said,
   "Quiet! Come out of him!"
The unclean spirit convulsed him and with a loud cry came
     out of him.
All were amazed and asked one another,
   "What is this?
A new teaching with authority.
He commands even the unclean spirits
   and they obey him."
His fame spread everywhere throughout the whole
     region of Galilee.

The Gospel of the Lord.

EXPLANATION OF THE READING

Every generation of TV viewers is familiar with the *Andy Griffith Show*. A notable contrast between Sheriff Andy Taylor and Deputy Barney Fife was their view of authority. Deputy Fife was all about "law and order," eager to jail anyone for what he perceived as legal violations. Sheriff Taylor, however, preferred the use of understanding, persuasion, and common sense. The people in today's Gospel passage were "amazed" because Jesus taught with "authority." He did not employ edicts, but told stories. He didn't just "say prayers"; he actually prayed and communed with God in a personal way. Don't we, too, crave authority rather than authoritarianism?

February 4, 2024

FIFTH SUNDAY IN ORDINARY TIME

A reading from the holy Gospel according to Mark   1:29–39

On leaving the synagogue
   Jesus entered the house of Simon and Andrew
     with James and John.
Simon's mother-in-law lay sick with a fever.
They immediately told him about her.
He approached, grasped her hand, and helped her up.
Then the fever left her and she waited on them.

When it was evening, after sunset,
   they brought to him all who were ill or possessed
     by demons.
The whole town was gathered at the door.
He cured many who were sick with various diseases,
   and he drove out many demons,
     not permitting them to speak because they knew him.

Rising very early before dawn, he left
   and went off to a deserted place, where he prayed.
Simon and those who were with him pursued him
   and on finding him said, "Everyone is looking
     for you."
He told them, "Let us go on to the nearby villages
   that I may preach there also.
For this purpose have I come."
So he went into their synagogues,
   preaching and driving out demons throughout
     the whole of Galilee.

The Gospel of the Lord.

Explanation of the Reading

No doubt you and I sometimes feel like Simon in this Gospel: "Everyone is looking for you!" We might have a crisis, a concern, a need, or a longing, but we cannot feel God's presence. Where is God? Jesus, off in a lonely place in the desert, perhaps suggests that God is already at work even when we cannot find him. Indeed, God is always with us. The seeking must be our work.

February 11, 2024

Sixth Sunday in Ordinary Time

A reading from the holy Gospel according to Mark   1:40–45

A leper came to Jesus and kneeling down begged him
    and said,
  "If you wish, you can make me clean."
Moved with pity, he stretched out his hand,
  touched him, and said to him,
    "I do will it. Be made clean." The leprosy left him
      immediately,
    and he was made clean.
Then, warning him sternly, he dismissed him at once.

He said to him, "See that you tell no one anything,
  but go, show yourself to the priest
  and offer for your cleansing what Moses prescribed;
  that will be proof for them."

The man went away and began to publicize
    the whole matter.
He spread the report abroad
  so that it was impossible for Jesus
    to enter a town openly.
He remained outside in deserted places,
  and people kept coming to him from everywhere.

The Gospel of the Lord.

Explanation of the Reading

From the beginning, Jesus steps out of line where human compassion is concerned. Both medical and ritual caution would advise him not to touch the leper. Jesus does not even hesitate when the man makes his confident request. The warning not to tell anyone, consistent throughout Mark's Gospel, is understandable if Jesus wants to achieve his aim to announce the nearness of the kingdom of God. Miracles reveal this truth but can also distract from it. Even today, many Christians are more interested in miracles and apparitions than in discipleship.

Lent

February 18, 2024

First Sunday of Lent

A reading from the holy Gospel according to Mark   1:12–15

The Spirit drove Jesus out into the desert,
   and he remained in the desert for forty days, tempted
     by Satan.
He was among wild beasts,
   and the angels ministered to him.

After John had been arrested,
   Jesus came to Galilee proclaiming the gospel of God:
   "This is the time of fulfillment.
The kingdom of God is at hand.
Repent, and believe in the gospel."

The Gospel of the Lord.

Explanation of the Reading

Mark's version of the temptation of Jesus in the desert is the shortest. Still, it evokes all the danger imaginable: a wasteland, angelic powers bad and good, wild beasts, and a lengthy time. Solitude and silence, even in a comfortable setting, can challenge heart, soul, and mind. One must believe that Jesus' retreat was a defining experience of his humanity. Only after his baptism and desert sojourn does Jesus proclaim with great conviction: "The kingdom of God is at hand." We need silence and solitude to deepen our faith convictions.

February 25, 2024

Second Sunday of Lent

A reading from the holy Gospel according to Mark 9:2–10

Jesus took Peter, James, and John
   and led them up a high mountain apart
     by themselves.
And he was transfigured before them,
   and his clothes became dazzling white,
   such as no fuller on earth could bleach them.
Then Elijah appeared to them along with Moses,
   and they were conversing with Jesus.
Then Peter said to Jesus in reply,
   "Rabbi, it is good that we are here!
Let us make three tents:
   one for you, one for Moses, and one for Elijah."
He hardly knew what to say, they were so terrified.
Then a cloud came, casting a shadow over them;
   from the cloud came a voice,
   "This is my beloved Son. Listen to him."
Suddenly, looking around, they no longer saw anyone
   but Jesus alone with them.

As they were coming down from the mountain,
   he charged them not to relate what they had seen
     to anyone,
   except when the Son of Man had risen
     from the dead.
So they kept the matter to themselves,
   questioning what rising from the dead meant.

The Gospel of the Lord.

Explanation of the Reading

Peter, James, and John witnessed a transcendent event that other followers did not. Such an experience is what Jesus' followers and opponents had been demanding. "Give us a sign!" The true Messiah, they believed, would show signs of glory and splendor. Jesus chose to downplay this expectation to prepare his followers for the scandal of the cross. Most would not accept it until after the resurrection. Even today, some Christians want to skip the cross and consider only the victory of Christ. The transfiguration, as private as it was, indicates that glory and splendor played their role in authenticating Jesus as Messiah.

March 3, 2024

Third Sunday of Lent

A reading from the holy Gospel according to John   2:13–25

Since the Passover of the Jews was near,
>   Jesus went up to Jerusalem.
> He found in the temple area those who sold oxen, sheep,
>   and doves,
>   as well as the money changers seated there.
> He made a whip out of cords
>   and drove them all out of the temple area,
>   with the sheep and oxen,
>   and spilled the coins of the money changers
>   and overturned their tables,
>   and to those who sold doves he said,
>   "Take these out of here,
>   and stop making my Father's house a marketplace."
> His disciples recalled the words of Scripture,
>   *Zeal for your house will consume me.*
> At this the Jews answered and said to him,
>   "What sign can you show us for doing this?"

Jesus answered and said to them,
   "Destroy this temple and in three days
     I will raise it up."
The Jews said,
   "This temple has been under construction
     for forty-six years,
   and you will raise it up in three days?"
But he was speaking about the temple of his body.
Therefore, when he was raised from the dead,
   his disciples remembered that he had said this,
   and they came to believe the Scripture
   and the word Jesus had spoken.

While he was in Jerusalem for the feast of Passover,
   many began to believe in his name
   when they saw the signs he was doing.
But Jesus would not trust himself to them
     because he knew them all,
   and did not need anyone to testify
     about human nature.
He himself understood it well.

The Gospel of the Lord.

EXPLANATION OF THE READING

International travelers know the inconvenience that exchanging currencies can entail. The Temple precincts were a currency exchange; coinage that represented a god or emperor was forbidden by the first commandment. Animals for sacrifice could be bought there with acceptable Jewish coinage. It is unlikely that Jesus would be offended by this practice. Rather, it was the corruption, greed, and malpractice in the name of God that often accompanied the business transactions that was reprehensible. John's Gospel account interprets this episode symbolically, as the beginning of worship in spirit and truth.

March 10, 2024

Fourth Sunday of Lent

A reading from the holy Gospel according to John   3:14–21

Jesus said to Nicodemus:
   "Just as Moses lifted up the serpent in the desert,
   so must the Son of Man be lifted up,
   so that everyone who believes in him may have eternal life."

For God so loved the world that he gave his only Son,
   so that everyone who believes in him
     might not perish
   but might have eternal life.
For God did not send his Son into the world
     to condemn the world,
   but that the world might be saved through him.
Whoever believes in him will not be condemned,
   but whoever does not believe has already
     been condemned,
   because he has not believed in the name
     of the only Son of God.
And this is the verdict,
   that the light came into the world,
   but people preferred darkness to light,
   because their works were evil.
For everyone who does wicked things hates the light
   and does not come toward the light,
   so that his works might not be exposed.
But whoever lives the truth comes to the light,
   so that his works may be clearly seen as done
     in God.

The Gospel of the Lord.

EXPLANATION OF THE READING

The evangelist John is a master at choosing words that have double meanings. In this passage and elsewhere, Jesus speaks of being "lifted up." This is a clear allusion to the cross upon which he would be raised up at his execution. It also means Jesus' glory, victory, his seat at the right hand of the Father. Among the evangelists, John shows clearly that the cross is Christ's exaltation. Looking upon it, we encounter the depth of divine love for us.

March 17, 2024

FIFTH SUNDAY OF LENT

A reading from the holy Gospel according to John   12:20–33

Some Greeks who had come to worship
    at the Passover Feast
  came to Philip, who was from Bethsaida in Galilee,
  and asked him, "Sir, we would like to see Jesus."
Philip went and told Andrew;
  then Andrew and Philip went and told Jesus.
Jesus answered them,
    "The hour has come for the Son of Man
      to be glorified.
Amen, amen, I say to you,
  unless a grain of wheat falls to the ground and dies,
  it remains just a grain of wheat;
  but if it dies, it produces much fruit.
Whoever loves his life loses it,
  and whoever hates his life in this world
  will preserve it for eternal life.

Whoever serves me must follow me,
> and where I am, there also will my servant be.
The Father will honor whoever serves me.

"I am troubled now. Yet what should I say,
'Father, save me from this hour'?
But it was for this purpose that I came to this hour.
Father, glorify your name."
Then a voice came from heaven,
> "I have glorified it and will glorify it again."
The crowd there heard it and said it was thunder;
> but others said, "An angel has spoken to him."
Jesus answered and said,
> "This voice did not come for my sake but for yours.
Now is the time of judgment on this world;
> now the ruler of this world will be driven out.
And when I am lifted up from the earth,
> I will draw everyone to myself."
He said this indicating the kind of death he would die.

The Gospel of the Lord.

Explanation of the Reading

Jesus finally announces his "hour." His audience thought this was the moment of revelation, when he, the Messiah, would truly act according to their expectations—namely, an insurrection and the overturning of Rome, albeit divinely ordered and led. Places would be traded—Israel would become the world's master; Rome and other greatpowers would be subservient. What a shock they received! Jesus speaks of hatred of one's life, service instead of domination, and glory associated with death. This is still a shocking message!

March 24, 2024

Palm Sunday of the Passion of the Lord

A reading from the holy Gospel according to Mark   11:1–10

When Jesus and his disciples drew near to Jerusalem,
   to Bethphage and Bethany at the Mount of Olives,
   he sent two of his disciples and said to them,
   "Go into the village opposite you,
   and immediately on entering it,
   you will find a colt tethered on which no one
      has ever sat.
Untie it and bring it here.
If anyone should say to you,
   'Why are you doing this?' reply,
   'The Master has need of it
   and will send it back here at once.'"
So they went off
   and found a colt tethered at a gate outside
      on the street,
   and they untied it.
Some of the bystanders said to them,
   "What are you doing, untying the colt?"
They answered them just as Jesus had told them to,
   and they permitted them to do it.
So they brought the colt to Jesus
   and put their cloaks over it.
And he sat on it.
Many people spread their cloaks on the road,
   and others spread leafy branches
   that they had cut from the fields.

Those preceding him as well as those following
> kept crying out:
"Hosanna!
Blessed is he who comes in the name of the Lord!
Blessed is the kingdom of our father David that
> is to come!
Hosanna in the highest!"

The Gospel of the Lord.

Gospel at the Procession with Palms.

Explanation of the Reading

The Lord's entrance into the city of Jerusalem stands in marked contrast to the way in which he moves among crowds throughout the Gospel accounts. He generally tries to downplay their attention, focusing hearts instead on the works of healing wrought by his hands. He instructs his disciples to avoid places of honor at banquets and to humble themselves at all times. Why then this exalted form of entrance, complete with palm branches and cries of "Hosanna"? Jesus wants to root kingship in his imminent suffering and death upon the cross. To die for the sake of the world is what it means for Jesus to be king. "Hosanna in the highest!"

Easter Time

March 31, 2024

Easter Sunday of the Resurrection of the Lord

A reading from the holy Gospel according to John 20:1–9

On the first day of the week,
   Mary of Magdala came to the tomb early
      in the morning,
   while it was still dark,
   and saw the stone removed from the tomb.
So she ran and went to Simon Peter
   and to the other disciple whom Jesus loved, and told them,
   "They have taken the Lord from the tomb,
   and we don't know where they put him."
So Peter and the other disciple went out and came
      to the tomb.
They both ran, but the other disciple ran faster than Peter
   and arrived at the tomb first;
   he bent down and saw the burial cloths there, but did not
      go in.
When Simon Peter arrived after him,
   he went into the tomb
      and saw the burial cloths there,
   and the cloth that had covered his head,
   not with the burial cloths but rolled up
      in a separate place.

Then the other disciple also went in,
> the one who had arrived at the tomb first,
> and he saw and believed.
For they did not yet understand the Scripture
> that he had to rise from the dead.

The Gospel of the Lord.

Explanation of the Reading

Today, like Peter running to the empty tomb, we greet our risen Lord and king. Our alleluias punctuate the air after our forty-day fast from them. We are clearly at the heart of the Christian high holy days. Yet if you ask a child what is the most important Christian holiday, you are bound to hear that it is Christmas. To counter this misunderstanding, we might sing our way into a renewed understanding of the importance of Easter. For example in the hymn the "Risen Lord," by Adele Clere Ogden, we sing "Hallowed, chosen dawn of praise, Easter, queen of all our days." Easter is truly the queen of the paschal mystery and the heart of the liturgical year. Let our alleluias never cease.

April 7, 2024

SECOND SUNDAY OF EASTER (OR SUNDAY OF DIVINE MERCY)

A reading from the holy Gospel according to John 20:19–31

On the evening of that first day of the week,
  when the doors were locked,
    where the disciples were,
  for fear of the Jews,
  Jesus came and stood in their midst
  and said to them, "Peace be with you."
When he had said this, he showed them his hands
    and his side.
The disciples rejoiced when they saw the Lord.
Jesus said to them again, "Peace be with you.
As the Father has sent me, so I send you."
And when he had said this, he breathed on them
    and said to them,
  "Receive the Holy Spirit.
Whose sins you forgive are forgiven them,
  and whose sins you retain are retained."

Thomas, called Didymus, one of the Twelve,
  was not with them when Jesus came.
So the other disciples said to him, "We have seen the Lord."
But he said to them,
  "Unless I see the mark of the nails in his hands
  and put my finger into the nailmarks
  and put my hand into his side, I will not believe."

Now a week later his disciples were again inside
  and Thomas was with them.

Jesus came, although the doors were locked,
    and stood in their midst and said, "Peace be with you."
Then he said to Thomas, "Put your finger here
    and see my hands,
    and bring your hand and put it into my side,
    and do not be unbelieving, but believe."
Thomas answered and said to him, "My Lord
    and my God!"
Jesus said to him, "Have you come to believe because you
    have seen me?
Blessed are those who have not seen
    and have believed."

Now, Jesus did many other signs in the presence
    of his disciples
  that are not written in this book.
But these are written that you may come to believe
    that Jesus is the Christ, the Son of God,
    and that through this belief you may have life
        in his name.

The Gospel of the Lord.

EXPLANATION OF THE READING

We find ourselves on the evening of the "first day," therefore Easter Sunday. The Lord appears to all the apostles except Thomas, who is absent. The Lord enters, greets them with shalom, and breathes the Holy Spirit upon them. Pentecost is fifty days after the resurrection, while in John's Gospel account, it is Easter itself. We might say this is the birthday of the Church. As Pope Leo the Great said, "Christ died that the Church might be born." Thomas will have to wait eight more days to encounter the risen Christ when he is moved from doubt to belief. He will move from empirical demonstration to true faith.

April 14, 2024

THIRD SUNDAY OF EASTER

A reading from the holy Gospel according to Luke 24:35–48

The two disciples recounted what had taken place
 on the way,
  and how Jesus was made known to them
  in the breaking of bread.

While they were still speaking about this,
 he stood in their midst and said to them,
 "Peace be with you."
But they were startled and terrified
 and thought that they were seeing a ghost.
Then he said to them, "Why are you troubled?
And why do questions arise in your hearts?
Look at my hands and my feet, that it is I myself.
Touch me and see, because a ghost does not have
  flesh and bones
 as you can see I have."
And as he said this,
 he showed them his hands and his feet.
While they were still incredulous for joy
  and were amazed,
 he asked them, "Have you anything here to eat?"
They gave him a piece of baked fish;
 he took it and ate it in front of them.

He said to them,
   "These are my words that I spoke to you while I was still
     with you,
   that everything written about me in the law
     of Moses
   and in the prophets and psalms must be fulfilled."
Then he opened their minds to understand
     the Scriptures.
And he said to them,
   "Thus it is written that the Christ would suffer
   and rise from the dead on the third day
   and that repentance, for the forgiveness of sins,
   would be preached in his name
   to all the nations, beginning from Jerusalem.
You are witnesses of these things."

The Gospel of the Lord.

Explanation of the Reading

Luke uses the expression "the breaking of the bread" both in his account of the Gospel and the Acts of the Apostles. Some scholars argue that this is a term for the Eucharist. Even if one disputes this, it is clear that the term refers to an action—breaking—and not simply to the bread. When we gather to break bread in any circumstance, it implies a friendly sharing. It is difficult to break bread with someone with whom we are quarreling, so it is no wonder that the first words from Jesus when he enters is "Peace be with you." Later in today's passage, Jesus eats a piece of fish in the disciples' presence, again demonstrating the collegial and peaceful nature of the meal.

April 21, 2024

FOURTH SUNDAY OF EASTER

A reading from the holy Gospel according to John   10:11–18

Jesus said:
 "I am the good shepherd.
A good shepherd lays down his life for the sheep.
A hired man, who is not a shepherd
 and whose sheep are not his own,
  sees a wolf coming and leaves the sheep
   and runs away,
  and the wolf catches and scatters them.
This is because he works for pay and has no concern
   for the sheep.
I am the good shepherd,
 and I know mine and mine know me,
  just as the Father knows me and I know the Father;
  and I will lay down my life for the sheep.
I have other sheep that do not belong to this fold.
These also I must lead, and they will hear my voice,
 and there will be one flock, one shepherd.
This is why the Father loves me,
 because I lay down my life in order
  to take it up again.
No one takes it from me, but I lay it down on my own.
I have power to lay it down, and power
  to take it up again.
This command I have received from my Father."

The Gospel of the Lord.

Explanation of the Reading

Pope Francis, in his encyclical *The Joy of the Gospel,* evokes the symbol of the Good Shepherd numerous times. Like Christ, who is the Good Shepherd, the Church goes forth as a community of missionary disciples, tending the ever growing flock. The Church desires to show mercy as the outcome of her encounter with God's infinite mercy. As Pope Francis notes in the encyclical, she is not afraid to get close to the sheep. He states, "Evangelizers thus take on the 'smell of the sheep' and the sheep are willing to hear their voice" (24).

April 28, 2024

Fifth Sunday of Easter

A reading from the holy Gospel according to John   15:1–8

Jesus said to his disciples:
  "I am the true vine, and my Father is the vine grower.
He takes away every branch in me
    that does not bear fruit,
  and every one that does he prunes so that it
    bears more fruit.
You are already pruned because of the word
    that I spoke to you.
Remain in me, as I remain in you.
Just as a branch cannot bear fruit on its own
  unless it remains on the vine,
    so neither can you unless you remain in me.
I am the vine, you are the branches.
Whoever remains in me and I in him
    will bear much fruit,
  because without me you can do nothing.

Anyone who does not remain in me
> will be thrown out like a branch and wither;
> people will gather them and throw them into a fire
> and they will be burned.

If you remain in me and my words remain in you,
> ask for whatever you want and it will be done
>> for you.

By this is my Father glorified,
> that you bear much fruit and become my disciples."

The Gospel of the Lord.

Explanation of the Reading

John presents us with the beautiful image of the Church as the vine and the branches. Baptism is the means through which each person is grafted onto Christ. This spiritual engrafting is accomplished by Christ's death on the cross. Therefore, we are in him and must abide in him. Apart from the vine, the branches cannot survive.

May 5, 2024

Sixth Sunday of Easter

A reading from the holy Gospel according to John 15:9–17

Jesus said to his disciples:
"As the Father loves me, so I also love you.
Remain in my love.
If you keep my commandments, you will remain
> in my love,
>> just as I have kept my Father's commandments
>> and remain in his love.

"I have told you this so that my joy may be in you
    and your joy might be complete.
This is my commandment: love one another
    as I love you.
No one has greater love than this,
    to lay down one's life for one's friends.
You are my friends if you do what I command you.
I no longer call you slaves,
    because a slave does not know what his master is doing.
I have called you friends,
    because I have told you everything I have heard
        from my Father.
It was not you who chose me, but I who chose you
    and appointed you to go and bear fruit
        that will remain,
    so that whatever you ask the Father in my name
        he may give you.
This I command you: love one another."

The Gospel of the Lord.

EXPLANATION OF THE READING

Jesus is the "face of God's mercy." Embedded in the Latin word for *mercy* is the word *cor*, meaning heart. Mercy is always an affair of the heart. When we talk about God's mercy, the Hebrew word *hesed* contains the idea of love and kindness. We are invited, then, to remain in God's loving mercy and kindness. Christ's message to "love one another" implies that we be kind and merciful to each other.

May 9 or May 12, 2024

Solemnity of the Ascension of the Lord

A reading from the holy Gospel according to Mark   16:15–20

Jesus said to his disciples:
   "Go into the whole world
   and proclaim the gospel to every creature.
Whoever believes and is baptized will be saved;
   whoever does not believe will be condemned.
These signs will accompany those who believe:
   in my name they will drive out demons,
   they will speak new languages.
They will pick up serpents with their hands,
   and if they drink any deadly thing,
      it will not harm them.
They will lay hands on the sick, and they will recover."

So then the Lord Jesus, after he spoke to them,
   was taken up into heaven
   and took his seat at the right hand of God.
But they went forth and preached everywhere,
   while the Lord worked with them
   and confirmed the word
      through accompanying signs.

The Gospel of the Lord.

Explanation of the Reading

The expression that both Mark and Luke use to speak about Jesus' disappearance from the earthly scene is "taken up into heaven." But in Acts it is simply "taken up," assuming to heaven. As Luke ends his Gospel with the Ascension, he begins Acts with the same event. In Acts, he is intent on bringing the disciples into the scene to demonstrate its importance for their future work. Luke is not presenting the story of the historical Jesus. He is more interested in conveying that the risen Lord has returned to the right hand of the Father, which is a prelude to the sending of the Holy Spirit.

May 12, 2024

Seventh Sunday of Easter

A reading from the holy Gospel according to John 17:11b–19

Lifting up his eyes to heaven, Jesus prayed, saying:
 "Holy Father, keep them in your name
  that you have given me,
 so that they may be one just as we are one.
When I was with them I protected them
  in your name that you gave me,
 and I guarded them, and none of them was lost
 except the son of destruction,
 in order that the Scripture might be fulfilled.
But now I am coming to you.
I speak this in the world
 so that they may share my joy completely.
I gave them your word, and the world hated them,
 because they do not belong to the world
 any more than I belong to the world.
I do not ask that you take them out of the world
 but that you keep them from the evil one.

They do not belong to the world
 any more than I belong to the world.
Consecrate them in the truth. Your word is truth.
As you sent me into the world,
 so I sent them into the world.
And I consecrate myself for them,
 so that they also may be consecrated in truth."

The Gospel of the Lord.

Explanation of the Reading

Having walked with the apostles in their missionary journeys all during the Easter season and having seen the tensions that existed in the early Church, especially between the Jewish Christians and the Gentile Christians, it is appropriate to pray for Christian unity. Jesus prays to the Father that all may be one as he is one with the Father and the Father with him. The same concerns that Jesus had for the early Church exist today when tensions arise among the Christian churches. Christian unity is a gift of the Holy Spirit. It is important to pray that the divisions that exist may be healed.

May 19, 2024

SOLEMNITY OF PENTECOST

A reading from the holy Gospel according to John   20:19-23

On the evening of that first day of the week,
   when the doors were locked,
     where the disciples were,
   for fear of the Jews,
   Jesus came and stood in their midst
   and said to them, "Peace be with you."
When he had said this, he showed them his hands
     and his side.
The disciples rejoiced when they saw the Lord.
Jesus said to them again, "Peace be with you.
As the Father has sent me, so I send you."
And when he had said this, he breathed on them
     and said to them,
   "Receive the Holy Spirit.
Whose sins you forgive are forgiven them,
   and whose sins you retain are retained."

The Gospel of the Lord.

John 15:26-27; 16:12-15 may also be proclaimed.

EXPLANATION OF THE READING

No matter our age or education or life situation, the Spirit can lead us to deepen our life in the Lord. Pentecost means that each of us possesses gifts that come from the Spirit and together those gifts enrich and build up the Body of Christ in the world. How will you serve him today?

Ordinary Time during Summer and Fall

May 26, 2024

Solemnity of the Most Holy Trinity

A reading from the holy Gospel according to Matthew 28:16–20

The eleven disciples went to Galilee,
  to the mountain to which Jesus had ordered them.
When they all saw him, they worshiped,
    but they doubted.
Then Jesus approached and said to them,
  "All power in heaven and on earth has been given to me.
Go, therefore, and make disciples of all nations,
  baptizing them in the name of the Father,
  and of the Son, and of the Holy Spirit,
  teaching them to observe all that I have commanded you.
And behold, I am with you always, until the end
    of the age."

The Gospel of the Lord.

EXPLANATION OF THE READING

Trinity Sunday follows immediately upon the heels of Easter Time to allow us to celebrate the nature of God. We believe in a God who is Three Persons in one Godhead—diversity in perfect community. Thus, the nature of God is the mystery of relationship. God's love is mutually given and received by the Father, the Son, and the Holy Spirit. Moreover, we believe that this love is so abundant that God freely shares it with the world: love begets love. Who God is provides insight into our human nature as well. We are meant to construct a community of diversity abiding in unity. We are meant to love without ceasing.

June 2, 2024

SOLEMNITY OF THE MOST HOLY BODY AND BLOOD OF CHRIST (CORPUS CHRISTI)

A reading from the holy Gospel according to Mark 14:12–16, 22–26

On the first day of the Feast of Unleavened Bread,
    when they sacrificed the Passover lamb,
    Jesus' disciples said to him,
    "Where do you want us to go
    and prepare for you to eat the Passover?"
He sent two of his disciples and said to them,
    "Go into the city and a man will meet you,
    carrying a jar of water.
Follow him.
Wherever he enters, say to the master of the house,
    'The Teacher says, "Where is my guest room
    where I may eat the Passover with my disciples?"'
Then he will show you a large upper room furnished
      and ready.

Make the preparations for us there."
The disciples then went off, entered the city,
   and found it just as he had told them;
   and they prepared the Passover.

While they were eating,
   he took bread, said the blessing,
   broke it, gave it to them, and said,
   "Take it; this is my body."
Then he took a cup, gave thanks, and gave it to them,
   and they all drank from it.
He said to them,
   "This is my blood of the covenant,
   which will be shed for many.
Amen, I say to you,
   I shall not drink again the fruit of the vine
   until the day when I drink it new in the kingdom of God."
Then, after singing a hymn,
   they went out to the Mount of Olives.

The Gospel of the Lord.

Explanation of the Reading

It has been suggested that Jesus used bread and wine in the celebration of the Last Supper because they are manufactured by a "paschal process," meaning that the ingredients in bread and wine must die in order to be fashioned anew. Bread comes from wheat that must be milled and baked. Wine comes from grapes that must be crushed and fermented. Both require human ingenuity. Each time you receive the Body and Blood of Christ, your "Amen" signals death to your former self to allow life in Christ to fashion you into something new. We give thanks for the mystery of the Eucharist in our lives and ask that our partaking in it be a genuine participation in the "paschal process."

June 9, 2024

Tenth Sunday in Ordinary Time

A reading from the holy Gospel according to Mark 3:30–35

Jesus came home with his disciples. Again the
     crowd gathered,
making it impossible for them even to eat.
When his relatives heard of this they set out to seize him,
     for they said, "He is out of his mind."
The scribes who had come from Jerusalem said, "He is
     possessed by Beelzebul,"
and "By the prince of demons he drives out demons."

Summoning them, he began to speak to them in parables,
     "How can Satan drive out Satan?
If a kingdom is divided against itself, that kingdom
     cannot stand.
And if a house is divided against itself, that house will not be
     able to stand.
And if Satan has risen up against himself and is divided, he
     cannot stand;
that is the end of him.
But no one can enter a strong man's house to plunder his
     property unless he first ties up the strong man.
Then he can plunder the house. Amen, I say to you,
all sins and all blasphemies that people utter will be
     forgiven them.
But whoever blasphemes against the Holy Spirit will never
     have forgiveness,
but is guilty of an everlasting sin."
For they had said, "He has an unclean spirit."

His mother and his brothers arrived.
Standing outside they sent word to him and called him.
    A crowd seated around him told him,
"Your mother and your brothers and your sisters are outside
    asking for you."
But he said to them in reply,
"Who are my mother and my brothers?"
And looking around at those seated in the circle he said,
    "Here are my mother and my brothers.
For whoever does the will of God
is my brother and sister and mother."

The Gospel of the Lord.

Explanation of the Reading

After the Solemnities of the Holy Trinity and the Body and Blood of Christ, we return to the "ordinal," or the "counting" Sundays in Ordinary Time. But the name of the season is derived from the Latin *ordo*, meaning "ordered" or "numbered" time. The rhythm of Ordinary Time reflects the rhythm of life—with its celebrations of anniversaries and its seasons of quiet growth and maturing. We must admit that no time is ordinary. Time is God's gift to us. What we do with our time is our gift to God.

June 16, 2024

Eleventh Sunday in Ordinary Time

A reading from the holy Gospel according to Mark   4.26–34

Jesus said to the crowds:
>"This is how it is with the kingdom of God;
>it is as if a man were to scatter seed on the land
>and would sleep and rise night and day
>and through it all the seed would sprout and grow,
>he knows not how.

Of its own accord the land yields fruit,
>first the blade, then the ear, then the full grain
>>in the ear.

And when the grain is ripe, he wields the sickle at once,
>for the harvest has come."

He said,
>"To what shall we compare the kingdom of God,
>or what parable can we use for it?

It is like a mustard seed that, when it is sown
>in the ground,
>is the smallest of all the seeds on the earth.

But once it is sown, it springs up
>and becomes the largest of plants
>and puts forth large branches,
>so that the birds of the sky can dwell in its shade."

With many such parables
>he spoke the word to them as they were able
>>to understand it.

Without parables he did not speak to them,
    but to his own disciples he explained everything
        in private.

The Gospel of the Lord.

EXPLANATION OF THE READING

Today's Gospel reading features the final two stories pointing to the reign of God in the collection found in this chapter of Mark. One turns on the everyday mystery of the growth of seed, and the other about the mustard plant shrieks with exaggeration and irony. Who in these stories is the farmer? Is it God or us? Perhaps, the farmer is Jesus, who will return at the second coming to bring in the harvest. But where is Jesus the farmer now, between the sowing and the harvest, when our days are marked by struggle and suffering, and we long for evidence of his presence? For this reason, we consider that the kingdom of God is both already but not yet.

June 23, 2024

TWELFTH SUNDAY IN ORDINARY TIME

A reading from the holy Gospel according to Mark 4:35–41

On that day, as evening drew on, Jesus said
    to his disciples:
  "Let us cross to the other side."
Leaving the crowd, they took Jesus with them
    in the boat just as he was.
And other boats were with him.
A violent squall came up and waves were breaking over
    the boat,
  so that it was already filling up.
Jesus was in the stern, asleep on a cushion.

They woke him and said to him,
   "Teacher, do you not care that we are perishing?"
He woke up,
   rebuked the wind, and said to the sea,
      "Quiet! Be still!"
The wind ceased and there was great calm.
Then he asked them, "Why are you terrified?
Do you not yet have faith?"
They were filled with great awe and said
      to one another,
   "Who then is this whom even wind and sea obey?"

The Gospel of the Lord.

EXPLANATION OF THE READING

How can it be that Jesus falls asleep, while his disciples fear for their lives, as the storm rocks the boat? Could it be that the Lord does not panic and worry about the things that fill us with anxiety? He faces the storm and calms the winds because his ultimate trust in God's will keeps him anchored, stable, and secure at all times. Jesus' sense of peace should be ours as well. We are able to ride the rocky waves of life when we believe that the mercy of God conquers even the greatest of our sins and failures. Place yourself in the boat with Christ, acknowledge the winds that disturb you, but then believe that faith provides for a smooth passage to new life.

June 30, 2024

Thirteenth Sunday in Ordinary Time

**A reading from the holy Gospel
according to Mark** 5:21–24, 35b–43

When Jesus had crossed again in the boat
   to the other side,
      a large crowd gathered around him, and he stayed close
         to the sea.
One of the synagogue officials, named Jairus,
      came forward.
Seeing him he fell at his feet and pleaded earnestly with
      him, saying,
   "My daughter is at the point of death.
   Please, come lay your hands on her
   that she may get well and live."
He went off with him,
   and a large crowd followed him and pressed
      upon him.

While he was still speaking,
   people from the synagogue official's house arrived
      and said,
   "Your daughter has died; why trouble the teacher
      any longer?"
Disregarding the message that was reported,
   Jesus said to the synagogue official,
   "Do not be afraid; just have faith."
He did not allow anyone to accompany him inside
   except Peter, James, and John, the brother of James.

When they arrived at the house
    of the synagogue official,
  he caught sight of a commotion,
  people weeping and wailing loudly.
So he went in and said to them,
  "Why this commotion and weeping?
The child is not dead but asleep."
And they ridiculed him.
Then he put them all out.
He took along the child's father and mother
    and those who were with him
    and entered the room where the child was.
He took the child by the hand and said to her,
    "Talitha koum,"
  which means, "Little girl, I say to you, arise!"
The girl, a child of twelve, arose immediately
    and walked around.
At that they were utterly astounded.
He gave strict orders that no one should know this
    and said that she should be given something to eat.

The Gospel of the Lord.

Longer form: Mark 5:21–43

Explanation of the Reading

Mark is very intentional in noting whom Jesus selects to accompany him on this journey of raising the dead girl to life. Jesus takes only the girl's mother and father with him into her room. This suggests familial intimacy around the girl's bedside. Jesus succeeds in raising the girl to new life and also, undoubtedly, in establishing a new household of faith in him—a family united in thanksgiving. Do you celebrate faith as a household, as the center of family life?

July 7, 2024

Fourteenth Sunday in Ordinary Time

A reading from the holy Gospel according to Mark 6:1–6

Jesus departed from there and came to his native place,
    accompanied by his disciples.
When the sabbath came he began to teach
    in the synagogue,
  and many who heard him were astonished.
They said, "Where did this man get all this?
What kind of wisdom has been given him?
What mighty deeds are wrought by his hands!
Is he not the carpenter, the son of Mary,
    and the brother of James and Joses and Judas
        and Simon?
And are not his sisters here with us?"
And they took offense at him.
Jesus said to them,
  "A prophet is not without honor except
    in his native place
  and among his own kin and in his own house."
So he was not able to perform any mighty deed there,
    apart from curing a few sick people
        by laying his hands on them.
He was amazed at their lack of faith.

The Gospel of the Lord.

Explanation of the Reading

The neighbors from Jesus' youth are probably willing to give him the benefit of the doubt as long as he doesn't say anything challenging. They seem to believe that the wise things he said were of divine origin ("What kind of wisdom has been given to him?"), yet they are unable to believe that such a great gift would be given to someone they know.

July 14, 2024

Fifteenth Sunday in Ordinary Time

A reading from the holy Gospel according to Mark   6:7–13

Jesus summoned the Twelve and began to send them out
> two by two
> and gave them authority over unclean spirits.
> He instructed them to take nothing for the journey
> but a walking stick—
> no food, no sack, no money in their belts.

They were, however, to wear sandals
> but not a second tunic.

He said to them,
> "Wherever you enter a house, stay there
> > until you leave.

Whatever place does not welcome you or listen to you,
> leave there and shake the dust off your feet
> in testimony against them."

So they went off and preached repentance.
The Twelve drove out many demons,
> and they anointed with oil many who were sick and
> > cured them.

The Gospel of the Lord.

Explanation of the Reading

Mark uses the expression "the Twelve" as synonymous with "the Apostles." Jesus gives his apostles both power and authority to speak and to act in his name. He commands them to do the work that he himself did—namely, to cast out evil spirits, to heal, and to proclaim the Word of God that they received from him. Jesus teaches that power and authority should be used for service to neighbor. The Lord entrusts each of us with gifts and talents for the building up of God's kingdom.

July 21, 2024

Sixteenth Sunday in Ordinary Time

A reading from the holy Gospel according to Mark 6:30–34

The apostles gathered together with Jesus
   and reported all they had done and taught.
He said to them,
    "Come away by yourselves to a deserted place
      and rest a while."
People were coming and going in great numbers,
   and they had no opportunity even to eat.
So they went off in the boat by themselves
     to a deserted place.
People saw them leaving and many came to know about it.
They hastened there on foot from all the towns
   and arrived at the place before them.

When he disembarked and saw the vast crowd,
   his heart was moved with pity for them,
   for they were like sheep without a shepherd;
   and he began to teach them many things.

The Gospel of the Lord.

Explanation of the Reading

The Gospel states that Jesus pitied the people, "for they were like sheep without a shepherd." He begins to teach and shepherd them. One can visualize that Jesus noticed immediately that the people needed care. They hastened to him because they longed for someone who would provide the attention and care they needed. Jesus likely noticed, too, that they could be led astray by some and fall prey to others. The image of Jesus caring for the people who followed him even to a deserted place is a poignant one. We can think of the care that our Lord has for us.

July 28, 2024

Seventeenth Sunday in Ordinary Time

A reading from the holy Gospel according to John   6.1–15

Jesus went across the Sea of Galilee.
A large crowd followed him,
   because they saw the signs he was performing
     on the sick.
Jesus went up on the mountain,
   and there he sat down with his disciples.
The Jewish feast of Passover was near.
When Jesus raised his eyes
   and saw that a large crowd was coming to him,
   he said to Philip,
   "Where can we buy enough food for them to eat?"
He said this to test him,
   because he himself knew what he was going to do.
Philip answered him,
   "Two hundred days' wages worth of food
     would not be enough
   for each of them to have a little."
One of his disciples,
   Andrew, the brother of Simon Peter, said to him,
   "There is a boy here who has five barley loaves
     and two fish;
   but what good are these for so many?"
Jesus said, "Have the people recline."
Now there was a great deal of grass in that place.
So the men reclined, about five thousand in number.

Then Jesus took the loaves, gave thanks,
    and distributed them to those who were reclining,
    and also as much of the fish as they wanted.
When they had had their fill, he said to his disciples,
    "Gather the fragments left over,
    so that nothing will be wasted."
So they collected them,
    and filled twelve wicker baskets with fragments
    from the five barley loaves
    that had been more than they could eat.
When the people saw the sign he had done, they said,
    "This is truly the Prophet, the one who is to come into
        the world."
Since Jesus knew that they were going to come
        and carry him off
    to make him king,
    he withdrew again to the mountain alone.

The Gospel of the Lord.

EXPLANATION OF THE READING

It is very interesting that in John's account of the multiplication of the loaves and the fish the source of the supply is a little boy. The one who is seemingly least significant and valuable in that large crowd of five thousand men is the one who provides the core material for Jesus' great miracle. Once again, this is a Gospel of reversal—Jesus chooses the assistance from the powerless to humble the mighty. Do not be surprised if God chooses to use you in a similar manner—out of your weakness, he may want to demonstrate something very powerful indeed.

August 4, 2024

Eighteenth Sunday in Ordinary Time

A reading from the holy Gospel according to John 6:24–35

When the crowd saw that neither Jesus
    nor his disciples were there,
  they themselves got into boats
  and came to Capernaum looking for Jesus.
And when they found him across the sea they said
    to him,
  "Rabbi, when did you get here?"
Jesus answered them and said,
  "Amen, amen, I say to you,
  you are looking for me not because you saw signs
  but because you ate the loaves and were filled.
Do not work for food that perishes
  but for the food that endures for eternal life,
  which the Son of Man will give you.
For on him the Father, God, has set his seal."
So they said to him,
  "What can we do to accomplish the works of God?"
Jesus answered and said to them,
  "This is the work of God, that you believe
    in the one he sent."
So they said to him,
  "What sign can you do, that we may see
    and believe in you?
What can you do?
Our ancestors ate manna in the desert, as it is written:
  He gave them bread from heaven to eat."

So Jesus said to them,
>"Amen, amen, I say to you,
>it was not Moses who gave the bread from heaven;
>my Father gives you the true bread from heaven.
>For the bread of God is that which comes down
>>from heaven
>and gives life to the world."

So they said to him,
>"Sir, give us this bread always." Jesus said to them,
>"I am the bread of life;
>whoever comes to me will never hunger,
>and whoever believes in me will never thirst."

The Gospel of the Lord.

EXPLANATION OF THE READING

Earlier in this chapter of John, Jesus fed a crowd of more than five thousand through the miracle of the multiplication of the loaves and the fish. But that miracle was not enough of a sign for the crowd to believe in Jesus. They want something more. It might be tempting for us to judge them harshly. But are not we the same in how we live our lives? Our market teaches us never to be satisfied, to always want something more. From the food we eat, to the clothes we wear, to the gadgets of technology that keep us company, we want more. Jesus tells us to come to him, and we will never want more, we will be completely satisfied.

August 11, 2024

Nineteenth Sunday in Ordinary Time

A reading from the holy Gospel according to John 6:41–51

The Jews murmured about Jesus because he said,
  "I am the bread that came down from heaven,"
  and they said,
  "Is this not Jesus, the son of Joseph?
Do we not know his father and mother?
Then how can he say,
  'I have come down from heaven'?"
Jesus answered and said to them,
  "Stop murmuring among yourselves.
No one can come to me unless the Father
    who sent me draw him,
  and I will raise him on the last day.
It is written in the prophets:
  They shall all be taught by God.
Everyone who listens to my Father and learns
    from him comes to me.
Not that anyone has seen the Father
  except the one who is from God;
  he has seen the Father.
Amen, amen, I say to you,
  whoever believes has eternal life.
I am the bread of life.
Your ancestors ate the manna in the desert,
    but they died;
  this is the bread that comes down from heaven
  so that one may eat it and not die.

I am the living bread that came down from heaven;
> whoever eats this bread will live forever;
> and the bread that I will give is my flesh for the life of the world."

The Gospel of the Lord.

EXPLANATION OF THE READING

Jesus declares that the bread that he gives is his flesh "for the life of the world." At the Eucharist, do we see ourselves participating in an action that is meant to ripple outward for the world's salvation? The components of the Eucharist are meant to form in us a pattern that brings life far beyond the church doors. We practice the art of "gathering," of "listening" to the Word, of "sacrificing" all that we are, to draw closer to one another in "communion." As you receive holy Communion, imagine yourself lifting the world up to the Father in Christ for its healing, bringing all people together in life.

August 15, 2024

SOLEMNITY OF THE ASSUMPTION OF THE BLESSED VIRGIN MARY

A reading from the holy Gospel according to Luke 1:39–56

Mary set out
> and traveled to the hill country in haste
> to a town of Judah,
> where she entered the house of Zechariah
> and greeted Elizabeth.

When Elizabeth heard Mary's greeting,
> the infant leaped in her womb,
> and Elizabeth, filled with the Holy Spirit,
> cried out in a loud voice and said,
> "Blessed are you among women,
> and blessed is the fruit of your womb.

And how does this happen to me,
>that the mother of my Lord should come to me?
For at the moment the sound of your greeting reached my ears,
>the infant in my womb leaped for joy.
Blessed are you who believed
>that what was spoken to you by the Lord
>would be fulfilled."

And Mary said:

>"My soul proclaims the greatness of the Lord;
>>my spirit rejoices in God my Savior
>>for he has with favor on his lowly servant.
>From this day all generations will call me blessed:
>>the Almighty has done great things for me
>>and holy is his Name.
>>He has mercy on those who fear him
>>in every generation.
>He has shown the strength of his arm,
>>and has scattered the proud in their conceit.
>He has cast down the mighty from their thrones,
>>and has lifted up the lowly.
>He has filled the hungry with good things,
>>and the rich he has sent away empty.
>He has come to the help of his servant Israel
>>for he has remembered his promise of mercy,
>>the promise he made to our fathers,
>>to Abraham and his children forever."

Mary remained with her about three months
>and then returned to her home.

The Gospel of the Lord.

EXPLANATION OF THE READING

Pope Pius XII proclaimed the Assumption of Mary an infallible teaching on November 1, 1950. This dogma holds that Mary was assumed body and soul into heaven. Mary's destiny is the destiny of the Church. It is our belief that, as members of the Body of Christ, we are destined for eternal participation in divinity. Like the woman in Revelation, the Church stands firmly planted in our world, confident that we will be "caught up to God and his throne."

August 18, 2024

TWENTIETH SUNDAY IN ORDINARY TIME

A reading from the holy Gospel according to John 6:51–58

Jesus said to the crowds:
"I am the living bread that came down from heaven; whoever
    eats this bread will live forever;
and the bread that I will give
is my flesh for the life of the world."

The Jews quarreled among themselves, saying, "How can this
    man give us his flesh to eat?"
Jesus said to them,
"Amen, amen, I say to you,
unless you eat the flesh of the Son of Man and drink his
    blood, you do not have life within you
Whoever eats my flesh and drinks my blood has eternal life,
and I will raise him on the last day.
For my flesh is true food,
and my blood is true drink.

Whoever eats my flesh and drinks my blood remains in me
>   and I in him.
Just as the living Father sent me
and I have life because of the Father, so also the one who feeds
>   on me
will have life because of me.
This is the bread that came down from heaven. Unlike your
>   ancestors who ate and still died,
whoever eats this bread will live forever."

The Gospel of the Lord.

Explanation of the Reading

Several years ago, Thomas Harris' character of Hannibal Lecter attracted much attention in two prime-time television shows. Many people were outraged at the very idea of a killer who feasted upon human organs. How did the Jews feel about Jesus saying "my flesh is true food, and my blood is true drink"? Certainly many people were outraged. This kind of talk continues to be problematic for people outside the faith. Jesus speaks so bluntly because he wants to be clear that union with him brings life. If we eat his flesh and drink his blood, then no aspect of our life can point to death; all that we are must herald new and abundant life

August 25, 2024

Twenty-First Sunday in Ordinary Time

A reading from the holy Gospel according to John 6:60–69

Many of Jesus' disciples who were listening said,
   "This saying is hard; who can accept it?"
Since Jesus knew that his disciples were murmuring
      about this,
   he said to them, "Does this shock you?
What if you were to see the Son of Man ascending
   to where he was before?
It is the spirit that gives life,
   while the flesh is of no avail.
The words I have spoken to you are Spirit and life.
But there are some of you who do not believe."
Jesus knew from the beginning the ones
      who would not believe
   and the one who would betray him.
And he said,
   "For this reason I have told you that no one
         can come to me
   unless it is granted him by my Father."

As a result of this,
> many of his disciples returned to their former way of life
> and no longer accompanied him.

Jesus then said to the Twelve, "Do you also want
> to leave?"

Simon Peter answered him, "Master, to whom
> shall we go?

You have the words of eternal life.
We have come to believe
> and are convinced that you are the Holy One of God."

The Gospel of the Lord.

Explanation of the Reading

In the midst of Jesus' teachings that bring us comfort and encouragement, there are those who challenge us. As the disciples said, "This saying is hard." Jesus doesn't apologize for these hard sayings. We shy away from lessons in life that are difficult; we would prefer the easy way to fulfillment. Our spiritual journey can sometimes be difficult. But we need to remember that we cannot do it alone. Only the grace of God sustains us in those times. Our faith may be tested at times, but the Lord assures us that he has the words of eternal life.

September 1, 2024

Twenty-Second Sunday in Ordinary Time

A reading from the holy Gospel according to Mark   7:1–8, 14–15, 21–23

When the Pharisees with some scribes
 who had come from Jerusalem
 gathered around Jesus,
 they observed that some of his disciples
  ate their meals
 with unclean, that is, unwashed, hands.
— For the Pharisees and, in fact, all Jews,
 do not eat without carefully washing their hands,
 keeping the tradition of the elders.
And on coming from the marketplace
 they do not eat without purifying themselves.
And there are many other things
 that they have traditionally observed,
 the purification of cups and jugs and kettles
  and beds. —
So the Pharisees and scribes questioned him,
 "Why do your disciples not follow the tradition
  of the elders
 but instead eat a meal with unclean hands?"
He responded,
 "Well did Isaiah prophesy about you hypocrites,
  as it is written:
 This people honors me with their lips,
  but their hearts are far from me;
 in vain do they worship me,
  teaching as doctrines human precepts.

You disregard God's commandment but cling
> to human tradition."
He summoned the crowd again and said to them,
> "Hear me, all of you, and understand.
Nothing that enters one from outside can defile
> that person;
> but the things that come out from within
> > are what defile.

"From within people, from their hearts,
> come evil thoughts, unchastity, theft, murder,
> adultery, greed, malice, deceit,
> licentiousness, envy, blasphemy, arrogance, folly.
All these evils come from within and they defile."

The Gospel of the Lord.

Explanation of the Reading

Jesus respected the many religious laws of the time but took issue with the attitude of those who kept the law for show and not from a sincerity of heart. Our spiritual life includes many visible postures, gestures, and actions. When they come from the heart, they express our true desire to serve others and please the Lord, they become vehicles of grace.

September 8, 2024

TWENTY-THIRD SUNDAY IN ORDINARY TIME

A reading from the holy Gospel according to Mark   7:31–37

Again Jesus left the district of Tyre
   and went by way of Sidon to the Sea of Galilee,
   into the district of the Decapolis.
And people brought to him a deaf man who had a
     speech impediment
   and begged him to lay his hand on him.
He took him off by himself away from the crowd.
He put his finger into the man's ears
   and, spitting, touched his tongue;
     then he looked up to heaven and groaned,
       and said to him,
   "Ephphatha!"— that is, "Be opened!"—
And immediately the man's ears were opened,
   his speech impediment was removed,
   and he spoke plainly.
He ordered them not to tell anyone.
But the more he ordered them not to,
   the more they proclaimed it.
They were exceedingly astonished and they said,
   "He has done all things well.
He makes the deaf hear and the mute speak."

The Gospel of the Lord.

EXPLANATION OF THE READING

Some of the healing stories from Jesus' ministry include unusual details. But these descriptions serve to emphasize the purpose of the evangelists—namely, to underline the astonishing power of God to alleviate human suffering. What is even more important is the reaction of the crowds. In their amazement they give praise to God, realizing that only God could restore life. In our time we are not often amazed; we believe we can figure everything out on our own. Such thinking blocks our seeing the hand of God in our life.

September 15, 2024

TWENTY-FOURTH SUNDAY IN ORDINARY TIME

A reading from the holy Gospel according to Mark 8:27–35

Jesus and his disciples set out
 for the villages of Caesarea Philippi.
Along the way he asked his disciples,
 "Who do people say that I am?"
They said in reply,
 "John the Baptist, others Elijah,
 still others one of the prophets."
And he asked them,
 "But who do you say that I am?"
Peter said to him in reply,
 "You are the Christ."
Then he warned them not to tell anyone about him.

He began to teach them
> that the Son of Man must suffer greatly
> and be rejected by the elders, the chief priests,
>> and the scribes,
> and be killed, and rise after three days.

He spoke this openly.
Then Peter took him aside and began to rebuke him.
At this he turned around and, looking at his disciples,
> rebuked Peter and said, "Get behind me, Satan.

You are thinking not as God does,
> but as human beings do."

He summoned the crowd with his disciples and said to them,
> "Whoever wishes to come after me
>> must deny himself,
> take up his cross, and follow me.

For whoever wishes to save his life will lose it,
> but whoever loses his life for my sake
> and that of the gospel will save it."

The Gospel of the Lord.

Explanation of the Reading

Peter acts in this story as many of us would. Jesus' forecast of the future seems like doom and gloom to the disciples. They must have felt he was just having a bad day, and so Peter tries to pick him up and encourage him. Jesus will have none of it. Sometimes we are guilty of trying to move people too quickly to a place of comfort without giving them the chance to make peace with their sin, their illness, their loss. Rather than listening to people work things out for themselves, we are quick to pose a solution to their problems, an easy way out of their dilemma. As Jesus suggests, however, the cross is burdensome and worthy of lengthy contemplation.

September 22, 2024

Twenty-Fifth Sunday in Ordinary Time

A reading from the holy Gospel according to Mark 9:30–37

Jesus and his disciples left from there
    and began a journey through Galilee,
  but he did not wish anyone to know about it.
He was teaching his disciples and telling them,
  "The Son of Man is to be handed over to men
  and they will kill him,
  and three days after his death the Son of Man
    will rise."
But they did not understand the saying,
  and they were afraid to question him.

They came to Capernaum and, once inside the house,
  he began to ask them,
  "What were you arguing about on the way?"
But they remained silent.
They had been discussing among themselves
    on the way
  who was the greatest.
Then he sat down, called the Twelve, and said to them,
  "If anyone wishes to be first,
  he shall be the last of all and the servant of all."

Taking a child, he placed it in their midst,
>   and putting his arms around it, he said to them,
>   "Whoever receives one child such as this
>   in my name, receives me;
>   and whoever receives me,
>   receives not me but the One who sent me."

The Gospel of the Lord.

Explanation of the Reading

Mark's contrast between Jesus' announcing his approaching act of humility on the cross and the disciples' argument about who was the most important, is stark and probably deliberate. It is worthy of our reflection: Why do we need to be important at all, let alone more important than others? Every bit of worth and dignity we have comes from God. We are rightfully proud—and important—only when we use our freedom to cooperate with God's grace and will.

September 29, 2024

Twenty-Sixth Sunday in Ordinary Time

A reading from the holy Gospel according to Mark 9:38–43, 45, 47–48

At that time, John said to Jesus,
>   "Teacher, we saw someone driving out demons
>   in your name,
>   and we tried to prevent him
>   because he does not follow us."
Jesus replied, "Do not prevent him.
There is no one who performs a mighty deed
>   in my name
>   who can at the same time speak ill of me.

For whoever is not against us is for us.
Anyone who gives you a cup of water to drink
   because you belong to Christ,
     amen, I say to you, will surely not lose his reward.

"Whoever causes one of these little ones who believe in
     me to sin,
   it would be better for him if a great millstone
   were put around his neck
   and he were thrown into the sea.
If your hand causes you to sin, cut it off.
It is better for you to enter into life maimed
   than with two hands to go into Gehenna,
   into the unquenchable fire.
And if your foot causes you to sin, cut if off.
It is better for you to enter into life crippled
   than with two feet to be thrown into Gehenna.
And if your eye causes you to sin, pluck it out.
Better for you to enter into the kingdom of God
     with one eye
   than with two eyes to be thrown into Gehenna,
   where 'their worm does not die,
     and the fire is not quenched.'"

The Gospel of the Lord.

Explanation of the Reading

True religion is pure and devoted to God. Unfortunately, religions have frequently betrayed their ideals, breaking into factions over teachings and interpretations. Pope Francis has made it clear that the pathway to God passes through one's conscience. In today's passage, John was distressed to see a good work performed by someone other than Jesus. At bottom, God's purpose in this world is peace, justice, reconciliation, love, community, and all good things. From whomever or whatever source, good is good.

October 6, 2024

Twenty-Seventh Sunday in Ordinary Time

A reading from the holy Gospel according to Mark   10:2–16

The Pharisees approached Jesus and asked,
   "Is it lawful for a husband to divorce his wife?"
They were testing him.
He said to them in reply, "What did Moses command you?"
They replied,
   "Moses permitted a husband to write a bill of divorce
   and dismiss her."
But Jesus told them,
   "Because of the hardness of your hearts
   he wrote you this commandment.
But from the beginning of creation, *God made them*
     male and female.
For this reason a man shall leave his father and mother
   and be joined to his wife,
   and the two shall become one flesh.
So they are no longer two but one flesh.
Therefore what God has joined together,
   no human being must separate."
In the house the disciples again questioned Jesus about this.
He said to them,
   "Whoever divorces his wife and marries another
   commits adultery against her;
   and if she divorces her husband and marries another,
   she commits adultery."

And people were bringing children to him that he might
> touch them,
> but the disciples rebuked them.

When Jesus saw this he became indignant and said to them,
> "Let the children come to me;
> > do not prevent them, for the kingdom of God belongs to
> > > such as these.

Amen, I say to you,
> whoever does not accept the kingdom of God like a child
> > will not enter it."

Then he embraced them and blessed them,
> placing his hands on them.

The Gospel of the Lord.

Shorter form: Mark 10:2–12

EXPLANATION OF THE READING

Are you prepared to "accept the kingdom of God like a child"? We tend to think that the more knowledge of God we accumulate, the more lovable we will be in God's eyes, or we are persuaded to believe that the more grace we build up, the more God will find us acceptable for eternal life. However, Jesus praises the children because they have none of that; they have no personal accomplishments that would make them stand out above others. This is how we must approach heaven—with the heart of a child. Take a moment to acknowledge yourself as a child of God, as completely dependent upon divine mercy rather than human resourcefulness.

October 13, 2024

Twenty-Eighth Sunday in Ordinary Time

A reading from the holy Gospel according to Mark   10:17–27

As Jesus was setting out on a journey, a man ran up,
>   knelt down before him, and asked him,
>   "Good teacher, what must I do to inherit eternal life?"

Jesus answered him, "Why do you call me good?
No one is good but God alone.
You know the commandments: *You shall not kill;*
>   *you shall not commit adultery;*
>   *you shall not steal;*
>   *you shall not bear false witness;*
>   *you shall not defraud;*
>   *honor your father and your mother.*"

He replied and said to him,
>   "Teacher, all of these I have observed
>   >   from my youth."

Jesus, looking at him, loved him and said to him,
>   "You are lacking in one thing.

Go, sell what you have, and give to the poor
>   and you will have treasure in heaven; then come,
>   >   follow me."

At that statement his face fell,
>   and he went away sad, for he had many possessions.

Jesus looked around and said to his disciples,
>   "How hard it is for those who have wealth
>   to enter the kingdom of God!"

The disciples were amazed at his words.

So Jesus again said to them in reply,
  "Children, how hard it is to enter the kingdom of God!
It is easier for a camel to pass through the eye
    of a needle
  than for one who is rich to enter the kingdom of God."
They were exceedingly astonished
      and said among themselves,
  "Then who can be saved?"
Jesus looked at them and said,
  "For human beings it is impossible, but not for God.
All things are possible for God."

The Gospel of the Lord.

Longer form: Mark 10:17–30

Explanation of the Reading

Like modern Christian preachers of the prosperity gospel, the man in the Gospel passage assumed that his material blessings were a reward for his knowledge and obedience to the Ten Commandments. However, Jesus perceived that material goods can fix our attention on this world. They potentially draw us away from God because they require attention, investments, and security. They define our social relationships. If personally earned, they incite pride and greed. The apostles were amazed at Jesus' remarks. They were not the first, and they will not be the last. We want to have both God and material goods.

October 20, 2024

Twenty-Ninth Sunday in Ordinary Time

A reading from the holy Gospel according to Mark 10:42–45

Jesus summoned the Twelve and said to them,
"You know that those who are recognized as rulers over
the Gentiles
lord it over them,
and their great ones make their authority
over them felt.
But it shall not be so among you.
Rather, whoever wishes to be great among you will be
your servant;
whoever wishes to be first among you will be
the slave of all.
For the Son of Man did not come to be served
but to serve and to give his life as a ransom for many."

The Gospel of the Lord.

Longer form: Mark 10:35–45

Explanation of the Reading

Having attended many ordinations through the years, I always remember a certain archbishop's annual misordering of the words from this Gospel: you have come to be served, not to serve. Of course, he corrected himself immediately. One might consider it a happy mistake, because it drew attention to our Lord's emphasis on serving. It is especially easy for people in power, including clergy, to grow accustomed to being served and fussed over. In the Church founded by Jesus Christ, everyone is a servant.

October 27, 2024

Thirtieth Sunday in Ordinary Time

A reading from the holy Gospel according to Mark   10:46–52

As Jesus was leaving Jericho with his disciples
    and a sizable crowd,
  Bartimaeus, a blind man, the son of Timaeus,
  sat by the roadside begging.
On hearing that it was Jesus of Nazareth,
  he began to cry out and say,
  "Jesus, son of David, have pity on me."
And many rebuked him, telling him to be silent.
But he kept calling out all the more,
  "Son of David, have pity on me."
Jesus stopped and said, "Call him."
So they called the blind man, saying to him,
  "Take courage; get up, Jesus is calling you."
He threw aside his cloak, sprang up, and came to Jesus.
Jesus said to him in reply, "What do you want me
    to do for you?"
The blind man replied to him, "Master, I want to see."
Jesus told him, "Go your way; your faith has saved you."
Immediately he received his sight
  and followed him on the way.

The Gospel of the Lord.

EXPLANATION OF THE READING

"Take courage; get up, Jesus is calling you." These words are addressed to the blind man, Bartimaeus, but they could easily be addressed to us. When we think about the call to discipleship, we tend to believe we have to be in the right place, having everything in our lives in order, our sense of self perfectly together. But this condition is not what Jesus is seeking. He searches for disciples who need him, disciples who are aware of their sins and weaknesses, disciples in need of mercy. This is Bartimaeus. He does not display great gifts that could be helpful for mission, other than the gift of his faith in Jesus. Let us come to the Lord with this faith that is seeking and crying out for mercy.

November 1, 2024

SOLEMNITY OF ALL SAINTS

A reading from the holy Gospel according to Matthew   5:1–12a

When Jesus saw the crowds, he went up the mountain,
    and after he had sat down, his disciples came to him.
He began to teach them, saying:

> "Blessed are the poor in spirit,
>   for theirs is the Kingdom of heaven.
> Blessed are they who mourn,
>   for they will be comforted.
> Blessed are the meek,
>   for they will inherit the land.
> Blessed are they who hunger and thirst for righteousness,
>   for they will be satisfied.
> Blessed are the merciful,
>   for they will be shown mercy.
> Blessed are the clean of heart,
>   for they will see God.

> Blessed are the peacemakers,
>> for they will be called children of God.
> Blessed are they who are persecuted for the sake
>> of righteousness,
>> for theirs is the Kingdom of heaven.
> Blessed are you when they insult you and persecute you
> and utter every kind of evil against you falsely
>> because of me.
> Rejoice and be glad,
>> for your reward will be great in heaven."

The Gospel of the Lord.

Explanation of the Reading

The Beatitudes must be understood in the light of the sovereignty of God or they don't make sense. After all, there is no comfort in grief, no heaven in being persecuted, and no reward in being insulted or slandered except in the perspective of God's kingdom. The saints are the men, women, and children who reflected the Beatitudes as individuals, who needed the Good News and found it, who knew the Good News and shared it, and who worked for the Good News at the personal cost of suffering and death. The saints, by their intercession, continue to assist us on earth as they help us find the Good News, share it, and bear its price.

November 3, 2024

Thirty-First Sunday in Ordinary Time

A reading from the holy Gospel according to Mark   12:28b–34

One of the scribes came to Jesus and asked him,
   "Which is the first of all the commandments?"
Jesus replied, "The first is this:
   Hear, O Israel!
   The Lord our God is Lord alone!
   You shall love the Lord your God with all your heart,
   with all your soul,
   with all your mind,
   and with all your strength.
The second is this:
   You shall love your neighbor as yourself.
There is no other commandment greater than these."
The scribe said to him, "Well said, teacher.
You are right in saying,
   'He is One and there is no other than he.'
And 'to love him with all your heart,
   with all your understanding,
   with all your strength,
   and to love your neighbor as yourself'
   is worth more than all burnt offerings and sacrifices."
And when Jesus saw that he answered with understanding,
   he said to him,
   "You are not far from the kingdom of God."
And no one dared to ask him any more questions.

The Gospel of the Lord.

EXPLANATION OF THE READING

The scribe's query continues to be relevant. The love of God is the supreme commandment. Unfortunately, some allow this fact to relegate charity and justice to second place. It should be clear logically that the love of God is the bottom line. A preacher might speak of addressing the needs of the poor; a listener might ask what this has to do with his spiritual life! The comprehensive love expressed by the scribe and affirmed by Jesus should inform every good work and every relationship.

November 10, 2024

THIRTY-SECOND SUNDAY IN ORDINARY TIME

A reading from the holy Gospel according to Mark   12:41–44

Jesus sat down opposite the treasury
   and observed how the crowd put money
      into the treasury.
Many rich people put in large sums.
A poor widow also came and put in two small coins worth
     a few cents.
Calling his disciples to himself, he said to them,
   "Amen, I say to you, this poor widow put in more
   than all the other contributors to the treasury.
For they have all contributed from their surplus wealth,
   but she, from her poverty, has contributed
     all she had,
   her whole livelihood."

The Gospel of the Lord.

Longer form: Mark 12:38–44

EXPLANATION OF THE READING

In ancient times, unless a widow had a male to support her, she was practically helpless. This is why giving to widows and orphans was an important religious practice for Jews. The widow who gave her two coins to the Temple treasury gave sacrificially, a sign of her piety and trust in God. Reason and prudence would have suggested that she hold back one coin for herself. She clearly illustrates the saying, "Give until it hurts!" She gave all and expected nothing in return. No doubt, many parishioners today give sacrificially, but there is often a demand for a return in services.

November 17, 2024

THIRTY-THIRD SUNDAY IN ORDINARY TIME

A reading from the holy Gospel according to Mark   13:24–32

Jesus said to his disciples:
"In those days after that tribulation
   the sun will be darkened,
      and the moon will not give its light,
   and the stars will be falling from the sky,
      and the powers in the heavens will be shaken.

"And then they will see the 'Son of Man coming
   in the clouds'
with great power and glory,
and then he will send out the angels
and gather his elect from the four winds,
from the end of the earth to the end of the sky.

"Learn a lesson from the fig tree.
When its branch becomes tender and sprouts leaves,
   you know that summer is near.
In the same way, when you see these things happening,
   know that he is near, at the gates.
Amen, I say to you,
   this generation will not pass away
   until all these things have taken place.
Heaven and earth will pass away,
   but my words will not pass away.

"But of that day or hour, no one knows,
   neither the angels in heaven, nor the Son,
     but only the Father."

The Gospel of the Lord.

EXPLANATION OF THE READING

As we approach Advent, end-time Scriptures become more regular in the Lectionary. Many believers, perplexed, ignore such passages. Others have taken them literally and with profound seriousness. As biblical commentator William Barclay wrote, these passages "were poetry, not prose . . . visions, not science . . . dreams, not history." Their core intention is to stress, through hyperbole, our accountability for our lives and for their ultimate fruits (or lack of fruit). We must hold on to the hope that Jesus will come again. The imagery is literary.

November 24, 2024

SOLEMNITY OF OUR LORD JESUS CHRIST, KING OF THE UNIVERSE

A reading from the holy Gospel according to John 18:33b–37

Pilate said to Jesus,
  "Are you the King of the Jews?"
Jesus answered, "Do you say this on your own
  or have others told you about me?"
Pilate answered, "I am not a Jew, am I?
Your own nation and the chief priests handed you over to me.
What have you done?"
Jesus answered, "My kingdom does not belong
    to this world.
If my kingdom did belong to this world,
  my attendants would be fighting
  to keep me from being handed over to the Jews.
But as it is, my kingdom is not here."
So Pilate said to him, "Then you are a king?"
Jesus answered, "You say I am a king.
For this I was born and for this I came into the world,
    to testify to the truth.
Everyone who belongs to the truth listens to my voice."

The Gospel of the Lord.

EXPLANATION OF THE READING

How willing are we to face the truth Christ has brought us? Pilate didn't want to face the truth. When he asked Jesus, "Are you the King of the Jews?" he was hoping that Jesus would deny the accusation. Instead, the truth had to be told, "My kingdom does not belong to this world." The truth brought Jesus face to face with the cross. The pattern of his kingship is that through suffering on the cross, God's glory is achieved. We will have to face the truth in our lifetimes—will the cross lead to death, or will it show us God's glory?

PATRON SAINTS

The saints and blesseds are our companions in prayer on our journey with Christ. Here we provide you with a list of health concerns and the saints chosen to intercede on a sick person's behalf before God the Father.

	ILLNESS	SAINT(S)
A	abdominal pains	Agapitus; Charles Borromeo; Emerentiana; Erasmus; Liborius
	abortion, protection against	Catherine of Sweden
	abuse victims	Adelaide; Agostina Pietrantoni; Fabiola; John Baptist de la Salle; Germaine Cousin; Godelieve; Jeanne de Lestonnac; Jeanne Marie de Maille; Joaquina Vedruna de Mas; Laura Vicuna; Maria Bagnesi; Monica; Rita of Cascia
	AIDS patients	Aloysius Gonzaga; Thérèse of Lisieux; Peregrine Lazios
	alcoholism	John of God; Martin of Tours; Matthias the Apostle; Monica; Urban of Langres
	angina sufferers	Swithbert
	appendicitis	Erasmus (Elmo)
	apoplexy, apoplexies, stroke, stroke victims	Andrew Avellino; Wolfgang
	arm pain; pain in the arms	Amalburga
B	babies	The Holy Innocents; Maximus; Nicholas of Tolentino; Philip of Zell
	bacterial disease and infection	Agrippina
	barren women	Anthony of Padua; Felicity
	barrenness, against	Agatha; Anne; Anthony of Padua; Casilda of Toledo; Felicity; Fiacre; Francis of Paola; Giles; Henry II; Margaret of Antioch; Philomena; Rita of Cascia; Theobald Roggeri

	birth complications, against	Ulric
	birth pains	Erasmus
	blind people, blindness	Catald; Cosmas and Damian; Dunstan; Lawrence the Illuminator; Leodegarius; Lucy; Lutgardis; Odila; Parasceva; Raphael the Archangel; Thomas the Apostle
	blood donors	Our Lady of the Thorns
	bodily ills, illness, sickness	Alphais; Alphonsa of India; Angela Merici; Angela Truszkowska; Arthelais; Bathild; Bernadette of Lourdes; Camillus of Lellis; Catherine del Ricci; Catherine of Siena; Drogo; Edel Quinn; Elizabeth of the Trinity; Germaine Cousin; Hugh of Lincoln; Isabella of France; Jacinta Marto; John of God; Julia Billiart; Julia Falconieri; Juliana of Nicomedia; Louis IX; Louise de Marillac; Lydwina of Schiedam; Maria Bagnesi; Maria Gabriella; Maria Mazzarello; Marie Rose Durocher; Mary Ann de Paredes; Mary Magdalen of Pazzi; Michael the Archangel; Our Lady of Lourdes; Paula Frassinetti; Peregrine Laziosi; Philomena; Rafka Al-Rayes; Raphael; Teresa of Avila; Teresa Valse Pantellini; Terese of the Andes; Thérèse of Lisieux
	breast cancer	Agatha; Aldegundis; Giles; Peregrine
	breast disease, against	Agatha
	breastfeeding women	Giles
	broken bones	Drogo; Stanislaus Kostka
C	cancer patients; against cancer	Aldegundis; Giles; James Salomone; Peregrine Laziosi
	child abuse victims	Alodia; Germaine Cousin; Lufthild; Nunilo
	childbirth	Erasmus; Gerard Majella; Leonard of Noblac; Lutgardis; Margaret (or Marina) of Antioch; Raymond Nonnatus

	childhood diseases	Aldegundis; Pharaildis
	childhood intestinal diseases	Erasmus
	children, convulsive	Guy of Anderlecht; John the Baptist; Scholastica
	children, death of	Alphonsa Hawthorne; Angela of Foligno; Clotilde; Conception Cabrera de Annida; Cyriacus of Iconium; Elizabeth of Hungary; Elizabeth Ann Seton; Felicity; Frances of Rome; Hedwig; Isidore the Farmer; Joaquina Vedruna de Mas; Leopold the Good; Louis IX; Margaret of Scotland; Marguerite d'Youville; Matilda; Melania the Younger; Michelina; Nonna; Perpetua; Stephen of Hungary
	children, sick	Beuno; Clement I; Hugh of Lincoln; Ubaldus Baldassini
	children, stammering	Notkar Balbulus
	colic	Agapitus; Charles Borromeo; Emerentiana; Erasmus; Liborius
	contagious diseases	Robert Bellarmine; Sebastian
	consumption	Pantaleon; Thérèse of Lisieux
	convulsions	John the Baptist; Willibrord
	coughs, against	Blase; Quentin; Walburga
	cramps, against	Cadoc of Llancarvan; Maurice; Pancras
	cures from pain	Madron
D	deaf people, deafness	Cadoc of Llancarvan; Drogo; Francis de Sales; Meriadoc; Ouen
	death	Michael the Archangel; Margaret (or Marina) of Antioch
	death, happy	Joseph; Ulric
	death, against sudden	Aldegundis; Andrew Avellino; Barbara; Christopher
	disabled, handicapped	Alphais; Angela Merici; Gerald of Aurillac; Germaine Cousin; Giles; Henry II; Lutgardis; Margaret of Castello; Seraphina; Servatus; Servulus

Patron Saints 227

	drug abuse	Maximillian Kolbe
	dying people, invoked by	Abel; Barbara; Benedict; Catherine of Alexandria; James the Lesser, Apostle; John of God; Joseph; Margaret (or Marina) of Antioch; Michael the Archangel; Nicholas of Tolentino; Sebastian
	dysentary	Lucy of Syracuse; Polycarp
E	earache, against	Cornelius; Polycarp of Smyrna
	epidemics	Godeberta; Lucy of Syracuse; Our Lady of Zapopan; Roch (Rocco)
	epilepsy, epileptics	Alban of Mainz; Anthony the Abbot; Balthasar; Bibiana; Catald; Christopher; Cornelius; Dymphna; Genesius; Gerard of Lunel; Giles; Guy of Anderlecht; John Chrysostom; John the Baptist; Valentine; Vitus; Willibrord
	ergotism, aginst	Anthony the Abbot
	erysipelas	Anthony the Abbot; Benedict; Ida of Nivelles
	expectant mothers	Gerard Majella; Raymond Nonnatus
	eyes, eye diseases, eye problems, sore eyes	Aloysius Gonzaga; Augustine of Hippo; Clare of Assisi; Cyriacus of Iconium; Erhard of Regensburg; Herve; Leodegarius; Lucy of Syracuse; Raphael the Archangel; Symphorian of Autun
F	fainting, faintness	Urban of Langres; Ursus of Ravenna; Valentine
	fever, against	Abraham; Adalard; Amalberga; Andrew Abellon; Antoninus of Florence; Benedict; Castorus; Claudius; Cornelius; Dominic of Sora; Domitian of Huy; Genevieve; Gerebernus; Gertrude of Nivelles; Hugh of Cluny; Liborius; Mary of Oignies; Peter the Apostle; Petronilla; Raymond Nonnatus; Severus of Avranches; Sigismund; Theobald Roggeri; Ulric; Winnoc

	fistula	Fiacre
	frenzy, against	Denis; Peter the Apostle; Ulric
	foot problems; feet problems	Peter the Apostle; Servatus
G	gall stones	Benedict; Drogo; Florentius of Strasburg; Liborius
	goiter	Blase
	gout, against; gout sufferers	Andrew the Apostle; Coloman; Gregory the Great; Killian; Maurice
H	hangovers	Bibiana
	head injuries	John Licci
	headaches	Anastasius the Persian; Bibiana; Denis; Dionysius the Aeropagite; Gerard of Lunel; Gereon; Pancras; Stephen the Martyr; Teresa of Avila
	health	Infant Jesus of Prague
	healthy throats	Andrew the Apostle; Blase; Etheldreda; Godelieve; Ignatius of Antioch; Lucy of Syracuse; Swithbert
	heart patients	John of God
	hemorrhage	Lucy
	hemorrhoid, piles	Fiacre
	hernia	Alban of Mainz; Condrad Piacenzai; Cosmas and Damian; Drogo; Gummarus
	herpes	George
	hoarseness, against	Bernadine of Sienna; Maurus
	hydrophobia (rabies)	Dominic de Silos; Guy of Anderlecht; Hubert of Liege; Otto of Bamberg; Sithney; Walburga
I	infectious diseases	Edmund; Rocco
	infertility, against	Agatha; Anne; Anthony of Padua; Casilda of Toledo; Felicity; Fiacre; Francis of Paola; Giles; Henry II; Margaret of Antioch; Philomena; Rita of Cascia

	inflammatory disease	Benedict
	intestinal diseases, against	Brice; Charles Borromeo; Emerentiana; Erasmus; Timothy; Wolfgang
	invalids, homebound	Roch (Rocco)
J	jaundice	Odilo
K	kidney disease, against	Benedict; Drogo; Margaret (or Marina) of Antioch; Ursus of Ravenna
	kidney stones; gravel	Alban of Mainz
	knee diseases or trouble	Roch (Rocco)
L	lame, the	Giles
	leg diseases, leg trouble	Servatus
	lepers, leprosy	George; Giles; Lazarus; Vincent de Paul
	long life	Peter the Apostle
	lumbago	Lawrence
M	mental illness	Benedict Joseph Labre; Bibiana; Christina the Astonishing; Drogo; Dymphna; Fillan; Giles; Job; Margaret of Cortona; Maria Fortunata Viti; Medard; Michelina; Osmund; Raphaela
	migraine	Gereon; Severus of Avranches; Ulbadus Baldassini
	milk, loss of by nursing women	Margaret of Antioch
	miscarriage, against	Catherine of Sienna; Catherine of Sweden; Eulalia
	miscarriage prevention	Catherine of Sweden
	muteness	Drogo
N	near sightedness, short sightedness	Clarus, Abbot
	nerve or neurological disease, against	Bartholomew the Apostle; Dymphna
	nursing mothers	Concordia; Martina
O	obsession	Quirinus
P	pain relief	Madron

	pandemic	Edmund the Martyr
	paralysis	Catald; Osmund; Wolfgang
	physical spouse abuse, against; victims of spouse abuse, against	Rita of Cascia
	plague, against	Adrian of Nicomedia; Catald; Cuthbert; Erhard of Regensburg; Francis of Paola; Francis Xavier; George; Genevieve; Gregory the Great; Macarius of Antioch; Roch (Rocco); Sebastian; Valentine; Walburga
	poison sufferers	Benedict, Abbot; John the Apostle; Pirmin
	pregnant women, pregnancy	Anne; Anthony of Padua; Elizabeth; Gerard Majella; Joseph; Margaret (or Marina) of Antioch; Raymond Nonnatus; Ulric
R	rape victims	Agatha; Agnes of Rome; Antona Messina; Dymphna; Joan of Arc; Maria Goretti; Pierina Morosini; Potamiaena; Solange; Zita
	rheumatism, arthritis	Alphonus Maria de Liguori; Coloman; James the Greater; Killian; Servatus
	respiratory problems	Bernadine of Sienna
	ruptures, against Osmund	Drogo; Florentius of Strasburg;
S	scrofulous diseases	Balbina; Marculf; Mark the Evangelist
	skin disease	Anthony the Abbot; George; Marculf; Peregrine Laziosi; Roch (Rocco)
	skin rashes	Anthony the Abbot; George; Marculf; Peregrine Laziosi; Roch (Rocco)
	sleepwalkers, sleepwalking	Dymphna
	smallpox	Matthias
	snakebite victims	Hilary; Paul
	spasms	John the Baptist

Patron Saints 231

	sterility, against	Agatha; Anne; Anthony of Padua; Casilda of Toledo; Felicity; Fiacre; Francis of Paola; Giles; Henry II; Margaret of Antioch; Medard; Philomena; Rita of Cascia; Theobald Roggeri
	stillborn children	Edmund
	stomach disease, stomach trouble	Brice; Charles Borromeo; Erasmus; Timothy; Wolfgang
	stroke	Andrew Avellino; Wolfgang
	struma	Balbina; Marculf; Mark the Evangelist
	surgery patients	Infant of Prague
	syphilis	Fiacre; George; Symphoroian of Autun
T	throat diseases, against	Andrew the Apostle; Blaise; Etheldreda; Godelieve; Ignatius of Antioch; Lucy of Syracuse; Swithbert
	toothaches	Apollonia; Christopher; Elizabeth of Hungary; Ida of Nivelles; Kea; Medard
	tuberculosis	Pantaleon; Thérèse of Lisieux
	twitching, against	Bartholomew the Apostle; Cornelius
	typhus, against	Adelard
U	ulcers, against	Charles Borromeo; Job
V	venereal disease	Fiacre
	verbal spousal abuse	Anne Marie Taigi; Godelieve; Monica
	vertigo, against	Ulric
W	whooping cough, against	Blaise; Winoc
	women in labor	Anne; Erasmus; John of Bridlington; Margaret (or Marina) of Antioch; Margaret of Fontana; Mary of Oignies
	women who wish to be mothers	Andrew the Apostle
	wounds	Aldegundis; Marciana; Rita of Cascia